'How unfair it all was! To arrive in the middle of an assassination!'

David Lindsay expected that his new employment with Cardinal Beaton would mean travel and the chance to enjoy fine clothes, pictures and architecture, music – all the things he felt were due to him. But on the first day after his arrival the Cardinal was murdered.

So whatever the rights and wrongs of the religious arguments between the Catholic supporters of three-year-old Queen Mary Stewart, and the followers of John Knox, the Calvinist, David had to think of more practical things. There was no way for him to get home to France. He was wounded, and his only refuge was the ramshackle hut belonging to the fisher-girl Elspeth and her grandmother, so he was completely dependent on Elspeth and what she could teach him. Through the long days of siege and plague in St Andrews he was drawn closer both to her and to the other townsfolk whose lives had been suddenly and dramatically changed by the religious war. And then, above all, there was the mystery of who Elspeth really was.

Iona McGregor, author of *The Edinburgh Reel* and *The Snake and the Olive*, has written a vivid story set in a stormy and absorbing period of Scottish history.

For readers of twelve and over.

IONA McGREGOR

The Popinjay

PUFFIN BOOKS

in association with Faber & Faber

Puffin Books, Penguin Books Ltd, Harmondsworth, Middlesex, England
Penguin Books, 625 Madison Avenue, New York, New York 10022, U.S.A.
Penguin Books Australia Ltd, Ringwood, Victoria, Australia
Penguin Books Canada Ltd, 2801 John Street, Markham, Ontario, Canada L3R 1B4
Penguin Books (N.Z.) Ltd, 182–190 Wairau Road, Auckland 10, New Zealand

—

First published by Faber & Faber 1969
Published in Puffin Books 1979

—

—

Made and printed in Great Britain by
Richard Clay (The Chaucer Press) Ltd, Bungay, Suffolk
Set in Linotype Baskerville

Contents

Historical Note

THE chief characters in this story are imaginary, but the public events in which I have involved them are well documented in various state papers and the sixteenth-century Scottish historians.

As these sources tell us very little about life in the city at this time, I have used the records of other Scottish burghs, the Baxter (i.e. Bakers') Books of St Andrews, and a mid-sixteenth century 'bird's-eye view' of the city, which shows a street-plan very little different from modern St Andrews.

The Castle was demolished after being captured by the French fleet, and the ruins seen today are mostly of a later date, but the 'secret passage' there has now been identified as the mine and counter-mine from the siege of 1546, and visitors can explore both.

Ordinary men and women of the time were not addressed as 'Master', 'Mistress', 'Widow', etc., and the Priory canons were known as 'Sir', rather than 'Father'. However, I have used these and other terms which were not common in sixteenth-century Scotland, as the correct forms are confusing for a modern reader.

CHAPTER ONE

The Cardinal's City

THE boy was as gaudy as a parrot in his blue velvet; the sun flashed off his rings and the brass pegs of his lute; and he flung back his head and sang insolently across the water while the sailors brought down the yards.

The sailors shouted and hauled on the creaking ropes, and the boy lounged against the deck-rail as he plucked his strings. He was playing a song they all knew, from the waterside taverns of Bordeaux. But the words were his own, full of French sailor slang, and meant for their ears, although he pretended to ignore them.

The words said that Orpheus of Greece had tamed the beasts on land, and Julius Caesar of Rome had tamed the pirates by sea, but there never had lived a god or hero who could endure the stink, the sloth, and the brutish stupidity of the sailors of the *Giroflée*.

The seamen scowled at what they understood. One of them managed to throw a rope-end near the boy. They did not dare to retaliate, for he was Monsieur David, son of the rich Scots wine merchant who had freighted the *Giroflée*. The voyage was nearly over; tomorrow they would be rid of the young gad-fly who had tormented them all the way from Bordeaux.

Soon the carrack lay at anchor with her sails furled, in St Andrews Bay. Up to the half-deck clambered a stout, puffing figure in brown doublet and scarlet hose, and stood beside the boy. Under the sandy beard, his plump cheeks were still green with seasickness.

'The tide's running out of the harbour. They have to lie at anchor until tomorrow.' He sounded fretful and disappointed.

Young David Lindsay frowned at the interruption. Master Reid had been much too familiar on their voyage from Bordeaux, as if he, David, were on a trading venture, too. He had shown the whole ship that he had nothing to do with his father's cargo, but Master Reid was slow-witted.

'How tedious,' said David.

St Andrews Bay was full of blue and golden light. There was no sound now but the faint swish of water as the carrack dipped gently between her cables. Across the water, tantalizingly near, lay the town and harbour, sheltered by the low Fife hills.

Last night, thought David incredulously, they had been pitching in a North Sea gale, and he had been so sick he had wanted to die. How he had cursed his father's Gascon wine! If those hundred barrels had not been ordered for the Cardinal's cellars, the *Giroflée* would have run for Leith harbour as soon as the storm blew up.

Above the huddle of thatched houses rose the city towers. His heart lifted to see them again: the college steeples of St Salvator's and St Leonard's, Holy Trinity Kirk, St Rule's, and the nine pinnacles of the cathedral. In the still, bright air, he could count the trees glistening in the Priory orchard.

Master Reid clutched the gunwale as if he still felt the planks bucking under his feet. 'Home,' he said with satisfaction. 'Och, well, what's another day on board? The sea's calm.' He gazed longingly at the shore.

A dozen three-masters lay at anchor near them. They had all missed the tide. Only a few small fishing-boats edged cautiously through the shallows towards their moorings.

On the edge of the cliffs near the harbour, the castle of Cardinal Archbishop Beaton rose straight from the sea. The Cardinal's banner glittered in the May sunshine.

'Has the Cardinal finished his new fortifications?' David asked.

'Nearly; they'd almost done with the second blockhouse when I left St Andrews.' Master Reid became solemn, because of the great name that had been mentioned. 'You'll see him the morn, then?'

David twirled the ribbon of his lute. 'Of course. His Chamberlain expects me.' His heart was hammering, but he was not going to let someone like Master Reid see his excitement.

It was only a year since he had left St Leonard's College, and only one month since the Cardinal's letter arrived to summon him back to St Andrews. He remembered his father's wry look as he read it.

'Maybe it means a place in his household, David. Still, great men are fickle. You'll come back to the wine-trade in the end. More sense in that than your Italian and Greek.'

His mother and sisters had sewn his new, gold-embroidered shirts, and his father had stuffed his purse with money.

'More sense in the wine-trade,' he grumbled, 'but you'll have to go. It's a great favour.'

David smiled, remembering his father's grudging pride.

He was nervous and excited, but he could not smirch his sixteen-year-old dignity in front of Master Reid. He would have to keep it all inside himself until he saw Martin.

He wanted to go on talking about the Cardinal, but there was only one piece of news to discuss, and that was unpleasant.

'Were you in St Andrews in March, for the – the burnings?'

Master Reid stiffened. 'I smelt the reek. I never went to look.' He eyed David cautiously. 'He was a good man, George Wishart, but he was daft to cast out with the Kirk. You dinna have any such notions yourself, I hope? Folk say St Leonard's men are becoming terrible Lutherans.'

David laughed. 'I've no interest in such things.'

'Nor I. I pay my tithes, and go to mass, and that's all. Folk should leave religion to the priests. Those Lutherans are fools. Where would St Andrews be without the Kirk? This is the Cardinal's city.'

A rowing-boat glided into sight, raising a small bow-wave on the blue, unrippled sea. It was making for the harbour and would come near the bows of the carrack.

Master Reid pointed excitedly. 'Here, let's go ashore. We can collect our trunks tomorrow. You'll stay at my house for the night.'

'I do not think –' began David distastefully.

'Nonsense,' cried the merchant, 'it's no bother at all. You've no friends or family near by, have you?'

'Only one friend in St Leonard's, and my cousins at Pitcairnie.'

That was almost true. His father's youngest sister was supposed to have come to St Andrews, many years ago, when she ran away from Pitcairnie with the leader of a pack-train. But that was an old scandal. He had never tried to find her.

'Pitcairnie's near the Lomonds. You couldna be back to St Andrews in time. Of course you'll bide with me!'

David bit his lips and muttered, 'Thank you.'

Master Reid went to tell the captain that they were leaving the ship and left David to hail the rowing-boat. As it changed course, he saw a pile of fish gleaming in the bows.

The rower lifted the blades and let them dip over the water. 'What d'you want?' she shouted. It was a girl about fifteen years old. She had a tangle of dark hair, and her ragged grey kirtle was hoisted to her knees. By her bare feet squatted a monkey with a tuft of bright red hair between its ears.

David stared down in amazement. The tiny skiff rocked up and down in the shadow of the carrack, and the monkey blinked its white-circled eyes.

'What d'you want?' repeated the girl impatiently.

Master Reid came back to the rail. He grinned and waved.

'Elspeth! ... It's the fisher-lassie that comes to dress my dinner,' he explained. He leant over the ship's side. 'Can you take us ashore?'

'Aye, if you hurry. The tide's far out. Make them let down a ladder.'

David went to the sterncastle cabin. He buckled on his rapier and dagger, slung his lute over his shoulders, and picked up his black velvet cap and perfumed gloves. In the doorway he hesitated. Then he went back to his chest that was lashed to the cabin wall and took out a large box of gilded leather.

'Good saints, do you need all yon gear for one night?' exclaimed Master Reid when he returned. David glared and, with the box clutched under his arm, climbed down the rope ladder.

The monkey huddled into the girl's skirts; she dipped her oars, and with smooth, neat strokes began to pull for the harbour. Master Reid offered no help, but she did not seem to need any. She looked stronger than most boys of her size. David edged his slashed velvet hose from the fishy thwarts. He was annoyed at having to make such an undignified entry into St Andrews.

'Was it a good trip?' asked the girl.

'Three barrels of prunes and walnuts, ten bales of silk. And that's not the half of it, Elspeth. I brought a fine Lyons velvet for the Gild altar in Holy Trinity. Not bad for my first voyage, is it?'

The girl's eyes glowed. 'Can I see the altar-cloth before you give it to the Dean of Gild?'

The merchant patted her sinewy leg. 'You can, and I've brought a wee present for yourself. But it will have to wait till the morn. What's your own news?'

'I cried into your house every day, like you asked.' The rhythm of her strokes faltered. 'Richard Strang has been miscalling you round the town. He tried to start a process with the bailies while you were away.'

Master Reid slapped the side of the boat. 'He's never stopped complaining since I first thought of giving up my bakehouse to become a merchant. I bought him out of his prenticeship and set him up with the Deacon. But he's as greedy as a hawk.'

He frowned for a moment, and then the girl said, 'Would you like some fish for your supper? They're fresh caught, and it's Friday.'

'Aye, thank you. Come up yourself and dress them for us.' David stared in outrage at the girl's brown hands, grimy with bait. She caught his eyes and held them steadily. David flushed and turned away.

At the harbour mouth the girl shipped her oars and then reversed one and used the butt-end to pole them through the shallows. She caught hold of a ladder nailed to the timber baulks of the pier.

'You'd best step out here. I canna bring you nearer the ramp, and you'll file your braw clothes if you walk over the mud.' Her eyes travelled derisively over David's velvet hose and gloves. 'I'll be up to dress your supper in a wee while.'

As they climbed up to the pier, she jumped into the harbour mud and began to drag her boat towards the wall. With a final disgusted grimace, David thrust her out of his mind, with all the shipboard noises and smells that had vexed him on the *Giroflée*.

They walked up the steps of Kirk Hill, past the Priory wall, and into Castle Wynd. Master Reid's house stood only one hundred yards from the castle.

Like its neighbours, it was timbered and thatched, with a forestair rising to the front door on the first floor. The stone-built cellars underneath were the bakehouse, and the outer wall of the stone oven had been carried up to form a chimney for the living quarters above. The house turned its gable-end to the street, and running beside it was a cobbled yard where the miller's cart could unload the flour for the bakehouse.

Master Reid pushed open the cellar door and lifted a huge iron key off its nail. 'I'm going to rebuild it all in stone and slates,' he said proudly. 'Just as soon as I sell my cargo and the Cardinal has finished with the masons. There's two of them bespoken to work for me next month. This bakery will make a grand warehouse. Then I'll not need to lease yon room down by the harbour.'

He straddled the cobbles and swung the key on his fingers. 'It was a hard decision.'

'Yes,' said David wearily. He had heard the story so often on the *Giroflée*. His lip curled. Soon he would be far above this city-burgess and his groat-grubbing concerns.

'I had to give over my craft when I became a merchant.

It's the law. This was the biggest bakehouse in St Andrews. I hired two journeymen myself and took in work for six master bakers. They were gey angry when I closed the bakehouse. I could have been elected Deacon of the Craft, last spring.' He sighed. 'It's the Corpus Christi pageant I'll miss the most. The bakers aye chose me to play St Cuthbert, because of my beard.'

David began to mount the forestair. Would the man never stop talking? He was longing to go to Martin.

Master Reid followed slowly. 'I did the right thing,' he cheered himself. 'Maybe the Cardinal will buy my silk for his pages' liveries. I can be on the Town Council next year. Maybe I'll be elected bailie. Then I could be Dean of Gild. Aye, I'll build it all in stone!'

Long swathes of golden light lay along the three streets that ran from west to east, towards the Cathedral. At eight o'clock the middens still steamed with heat, and the street was full of people, pigs, and scrounging dogs.

David elbowed through the crowd with the gilded leather box under his arm; but he suddenly found himself alone on the crown of the causeway. The crowd had fallen back to the gutters and the dogs yelped as they were kicked out of the way.

A respectful silence fell on the street. David stepped quickly to the wall. Along came a strange group: three gentlemen-in-waiting in crimson velvet, and six men who looked like tailors. Each of these carried a cushion or a wooden cross, and upon them, stiff with jewels and gold thread, hung or lay a pair of gloves, Turkish slippers, an embroidered cope, and a bishop's mitre.

The nine bearers walked as gravely as priests in a procession. No one seemed to think it strange that the Cardinal's new vestments should be carried through the streets, and David saw some of the women kneel down and cross themselves as if they had been looking at a holy relic.

Then the procession was gone; the people stirred, and a gang of screaming children whirled round the middens, playing football with a pig's bladder.

As he passed the west door of the Cathedral, David heard the tolling of Elizabeth, St Leonard's bell. The sound almost sent him running to the chapel, where he had been late on so many evenings. At the gateway he sniffed for the smell of *brodium,* the vile stew they had for supper.

O invisum brodium,
Quantum moves odium!

He grinned as he repeated the doggerel the students used to chant, beating their horn spoons on the table, if the stew was more burnt than usual.

Today, however, was Friday: they would be eating fish. And he no longer belonged here. He must see Martin before the gates were shut.

The face in the porter's lodge was new. David strode through with a wave of his hand. No English could be spoken inside the College, and his colloquial Latin was rusty. Pursued by an indignant '*Heus, tu*!' he ran up the narrow stone stair to the first floor.

The room he had shared with Martin looked over the College gardens to the Kinness Burn. It was like all the others: a small stone cell with one bed and a table. But an apple-tree grew outside the window, full of birds in summer, and good for swarming down to beat the curfew, in the early nights of winter. David smiled as he pushed open the door.

Something inside him twisted as he saw a stranger's books and clothes jumbled beside Martin's. But the stranger had not replaced him entirely; Martin's clubs and the pile of little brown balls stood alone, except for David's own two clubs he had given him when he went away. No one in Bordeaux played the Scottish game of golf.

He settled down to wait by the window. The College garden was white with sheets spread out to dry. The old laundress (the only woman allowed into the College) was moving round like a huge moth, gathering them into a wicker basket.

He was just going to call out to her when the door creaked. Martin blinked short-sightedly at him, and then his arms came forward in an awkward, joyful gesture. 'David!'

David grinned with delight. '*Maxime gaudeo, mi amice, quod –*'

Martin thumped him on the shoulder.

'Leave yon priests' gabble. I thought you'd be another month at least.'

'Well, here I am. What's he like? The one you share with.' David nodded at the pile of books on the bed. It was strange to be talking English to Martin. They had never used it, except for some hurried words on the links, when the College Regent was out of earshot.

'He's all right. He comes from Dundee. I sleep better now – he's not so long in the legs as you.'

They laughed together, and Martin pulled at the slashings on David's blue velvet doublet. 'Popinjay!' he said sardonically. 'No wonder we called you that. You're more of a Frenchman than ever. You've almost got a beard, too, but you're as fair as a lassie, and it doesna show.' He wrinkled his nose. 'Fooh! You stink of musk,' he growled.

The insults were a sign of affection. David let him finish before he gave his news.

'You don't know why I'm here.' He paused for effect. 'The Cardinal has sent for me.'

Martin, who had thrown himself on the bed, sat up abruptly. 'You're not going into his service!'

For a moment David convinced himself that Martin's long face had become rigid with admiration. 'Yes, but I won't accept a post in Scotland. He sends envoys to the Vatican and the courts of the Italian princes. Think of the libraries, Martin, and the jewels, and the paintings – and the beautiful women!'

'Maybe he'll not send you to Italy,' said Martin heavily.

'Perhaps he'll give me the revenues of an abbey or priory. Half the younger sons in Scotland live that way. Only a small one, of course.' The joke fell lamely.

'Why *you*?' asked Martin fiercely.

'Why not? My father has shipped the Cardinal's wines ever since he was Abbot of Arbroath. I am named after the Cardinal, and he gave me my scholar's place at St Leonard's.'

'Aye, before the right age. And you cast it over after a year,' reminded Martin. His face brooded.

David shrugged. 'I didn't learn anything more than I'd already learnt in Bordeaux, at the College de Guyenne. If I get an abbey, Martin, you shall be my sub-prior.'

Martin grinned sourly. 'So that you can jaunt off and dally with the lassies in Italy? Well, it'll have to bide till after tomorrow. I have to wait on Norman Leslie.' His voice became angry. 'The high and mighty Master of Rothes. My mother's lease falls in this year. You ken she has a bit farm from him near Lindores. So I maunna anger him. When he's here I have to run his messages, almost tie his points for him!'

David laughed. 'Why wait for Norman to fling you a bone? I'll speak for you to the Cardinal.'

It was half a joke, and half a promise. Martin sprang off the bed and gripped David's arm. 'You'll do no such thing!'

David was too surprised to be angry, and Martin backed away, muttering, 'I'm sorry, David.'

David looked at his friend in silence. In the College disputations, Martin was a word-spinner, moving deftly among ideas and abstract Latin phrases. In all other matters he shambled like a bear. His clumsy tongue had lost him many friends. David tried to distract him. He unclasped his gilded leather case.

'I want to show you something. My father told me to bring a present for the Cardinal.'

Martin, eager to be forgiven, lifted his head.

From the red silk folds inside the case, David lifted a Venetian glass goblet. It was so beautiful, his hands shook as he unwrapped it. He held it to the waning light, entranced.

'Very bonny,' said Martin indifferently.

David's throat tightened with disappointment. He put the goblet away. Martin seemed to feel he had to justify himself and folded his arms aggressively.

'Fine gee-gaws for the lassies! I dinna doubt the Cardinal can find a use for it.'

David flushed with vexation. Martin was as uncouth, he thought, as the sailors on the *Giroflée*. He turned towards the door.

'Maybe I'll see you in the Castle tomorrow,' said Martin gruffly. 'Norman and the Treasurer's son are taking a petition to the Cardinal. He's to ask the Cardinal to let us read Tyndale's English Testament again.'

David stopped in astonishment. 'The Pope has banned it for heresy!'

'The English can read the Bible in their own tongue.

We had the English Testament here for six months, before the Frenchmen at court and the Cardinal's priests stopped us.'

'The King of England is a heretic,' persisted David. He was not interested in the argument, but he was annoyed with Martin. There had been so much of this in Bordeaux: fierce ranting and discussion between the Scots merchants at his father's table, ever since King James the Fifth of Scots had died and left his throne to a little girl who was now only three years old. The 'English Party' wanted to marry her to the Prince of Wales; the 'French Party' and her French mother wanted to send her to France. It was all supremely boring.

'You know I don't take sides in politics,' said David.

'No,' agreed Martin with contempt. 'You have no more sense of public affairs than a woman.'

David winced, but tried to take it as a joke. 'You're becoming a bonny Lutheran. Mind you don't scorch your fingers. Hasn't the Cardinal quarrelled with Norman Leslie and his father? He won't grant your petition.'

'We shall make him ... Will you come to see me to-morrow, David?'

'Of course. Look, I can hear the porter's bell. Good-bye.'

He ran down the stairs whistling, but he felt uneasy. He had heard Martin criticize the priests before – who didn't? His father said that one must laugh at the bad clergy, be thankful for the good ones, and put up with the rest, who were men like oneself. The Church was the Church; only a fool would rush into the flames.

He was sorry that Martin had become so serious. Regretfully, he thought of all the things he had meant to ask him: had he found a stroke to beat that bunker they had nicknamed King Arthur's Cave? Was the fat canon at the

Priory still trying to grow artichokes? What had happened to the poor student who was caught last year eating the College candles?

As he walked back to Castle Wynd his fears began to seem foolish in the quiet summer evening. The sky was the colour of his Venetian goblet, an opaque, milky green; lanterns were already hanging on the forestairs of the houses. The gate of Master Reid's garden stood open. David slipped inside, drawn by the scent of herbs on which the dew was beginning to settle. He crushed a stem of thyme and held it to his nose. At this hour his mother would walk through the herb garden at home with Berthe the cook, talking to her in a mixture of French and Scots that no one else could understand.

There was a flash of scarlet by the pear-tree at the end of the garden. David saw Master Reid step back from the tree in a swirl of white wings, as half a dozen doves fluttered down to his shoulders and outstretched arms.

'There, my honeys,' said Master Reid, in a soft, croodling voice. 'Why are you not with the others?' The doves answered with a gentle croak and stirring of their throat-feathers. He carried them to a stone hut built like a bee-hive against the garden-dyke. Very gently, he lifted them one by one and patted them towards the openings in the stone roof. When they were all inside the dove-cot, he listened for a moment to make sure that they had settled, and then he began to walk on tiptoe up the garden path.

CHAPTER TWO

'There, There, is Your God'

BEFORE dawn David swallowed some bread and ale in Master Reid's kitchen; he was too restless to stay in bed longer. It was an unseemly time to knock at the Castle gates, so he walked down Kirk Hill to the harbour, and looked at the gaunt skerries of rock running into the grey sea.

The tide had come in during darkness, and was on the ebb again. The tall three-masters still rode at anchor in the bay. There was no one on the quay except a beggar dozing by the customs house on a pile of nets.

David timed his impatient steps by the maddening tinkle of bells from the Priory and other chapels in the town. Would the sun never rise?

As he faced the empty harbour, where the Kinness Burn trickled through in an oily stream, he saw the girl who had rowed him ashore from the *Giroflée*. She was jabbing a stick into the mud for bait. Behind her shambled the red-crested monkey.

David remembered that the girl had come to cook their supper with well-scrubbed hands, and had baked the fish in wine and herbs. He felt generous; besides, Master Reid had not paid her for rowing them ashore. He unknotted the silk cords of his purse and took out a silver groat. With a loud whistle, he flicked it across the muddy harbour.

It glittered for an instant by the girl's bare toes; then the monkey scooped it up. The girl straightened herself with a startled look. She snatched the groat, spat on it, and rubbed it clean. David flourished his cap, and smiled, ready for her thanks.

The girl looked very annoyed. Her arm jerked back, and she spun the groat across the burn. It ran tinkling along the quay, and the girl returned to her bait-collecting.

The beggar sniggered behind David. He clenched his rapier-hilt, choking with mortification. Then he shrugged. She was an ignorant fisher-girl, too stupid to appreciate his kindness. He would not give her another chance. He strode away magnificently, and the old beggar shuffled forward on his knees, and swept the coin into his wooden bowl.

The sun had laid a dazzling path across the sea when David reached the Castle forecourt. The gates were still shut, and a group of workmen waited outside with their carts. They were full of sand and lime, and the great blocks of dressed stone for the last course of the eastern blockhouse. The tower was still covered with scaffolding, but the guns were already in position. The wooden shutters of the gun-ports were open, and inside, bronze cannon raked the road to east and west.

The sun glinted on the sea, and a chilly breeze swirled a cloud of lime-dust round the carts. The oxen bellowed in discomfort, and David, frowning, brushed his doublet and the gilded leather case.

One of the masons flicked his leather apron in imitation. 'You'll have to wait like us, laddie,' he mocked, and the others guffawed.

David walked away to the furthest corner of the yard. Wait with them? Foul-nailed journeymen, insolent jack-peasants! His ears burnt at the jokes passed behind his stiff back, but he did not turn round as he heard the gates creak open. He would not give them the chance to jostle him in the entrance. He would let them go through before he went to the Chamberlain.

When he looked round the last cart was trundling across the bridge that spanned the ditch, and the porter leant against the gateway, swinging his keys. Some young men crossed the yard in front of David, all dressed in leather jacks or breastplates, wearing plain, heavy swords. Behind them sauntered a short, thick-set man with glossy black hair and red cheeks. From a distance, he looked like a plump fourteen-year-old boy. David recognized Norman Leslie, the Master of Rothes.

He stared with interest. He knew a few of Leslie's companions. They were the sons of Fife lairds, and some of them had been his fellow-students. He had gone hawking with them along the Eden.

'They'd do better with their petition if they bought some new hose,' he sneered. There was no sign of Martin. He strolled towards the group, wondering what to do. He was not sure that he wanted to kiss the Cardinal's ring in the company of such badly dressed hobbledehoys.

'No, his Eminence is not yet out of bed,' he heard the porter say. The men did not seem in any hurry to enter. Two of them began to talk to the porter about the new fortifications, and Norman Leslie lounged against one of the huge, studded doors.

His eyes narrowed as he saw David. 'Young Pitcairnie's cousin,' he said softly. He looked at the gilded box. 'You're a goldsmith's prentice now, are you?'

'I have the Cardinal's command to present myself,' said David stiffly.

Leslie's arrogant mouth opened a little. 'Have you, now?'

The porter stood in the gateway. 'Sirs, I'm sorry. I've orders to close the gates as soon as the masons are in.'

There was a murmur from the young men; they looked at Norman Leslie. He smiled and straddled the footbridge. 'Surely the Cardinal will see us.'

'You must come later, sir. Please stand back.' The porter heaved at one of the enormous doors.

Leslie strode forward and threw an arm round David's shoulders. He was half a head shorter, but as strong as a bull. 'Master David shall be our pass. Will you not, laddie?'

David pulled himself away and, without speaking, presented the Cardinal's letter to the porter. The porter inspected the seal. 'Right. Come you in, sir.'

'And us, too,' said Leslie. 'Sandy Skirling, do you want to open your gates twice? We shall be back.'

The porter stood aside reluctantly. 'Och, very well. But dinna blame me if you're cooling your heels for half the day. You'll need to ask the Chamberlain.'

The archway was long and dark, and David had the impression that at least fifteen men surrounded him. They were strangely silent; there was no sound but the echo of their footsteps in the passage. David glanced uneasily at their set faces. No one but Norman had greeted him.

He had nearly reached the inner courtyard when he heard angry voices behind him. Turning round, he saw someone else on the bridge: an older man, grim-faced, with a short grey beard. It was John Leslie, Norman's uncle, notorious for his hatred of the Cardinal.

The porter barred the way nervously. 'You canna come through, sir.'

The men spread themselves across the passage and Norman gave a quick nod to his uncle. John Leslie brushed his steel gauntlet across the porter's face. Two men snatched the porter's keys and two more stifled his shouts.

'More, you fools,' said John Leslie. Someone smashed the bunch of keys acrosss the porter's head. He grunted and slumped on the cobbles. They threw his body into the ditch.

For a moment David was paralysed with horror. Then he struggled out of the crowd and ran towards the inner courtyard. Perhaps they had stunned the porter out of brutal rage. But in his heart he knew that there was more to come.

There were cries behind him. 'Quiet!' hissed Norman. His grip was round David's throat, and forced him to his knees. Norman whispered urgently. 'You two! Hold him still, but dinna harm him. He's Lindsay of Pitcairnie's cousin.'

They dragged David to a stone bench facing the well. One of them kept his glove pressed against David's teeth; it tasted of greasy leather and horse-sweat. The gilded case was still clutched under his right arm.

He watched Norman Leslie stand under the archway, and with signs and whispers send his men to the apartments round the inner courtyard. There was no sound but the tramp of their feet on the cobbles.

The masons were cleared off the walls and pushed through the gate with the flat of Norman's sword. They trooped away in bewildered silence.

Then, one by one, the Cardinal's attendants were dragged from their rooms in the north wing. They came out chattering excitedly in French, until they were beaten into silence. Some of them were in shirt-sleeves, and others had their half-trussed hose falling to their knees. One man clutched a sheet round him.

After they had gone there was an expectant silence in the courtyard. The sixteen looked at each other.

'Fine,' said Norman quietly. 'Fetch cross-bows from the armoury. Put the men-at-arms outside. Then close the gates.'

Soon about fifty soldiers filed from a doorway in the west wing. They were unarmed, but there were only ten men in front of them. 'They'll run at them,' thought David. 'They could knock them down in a minute.'

But the men-at-arms let themselves be herded to the gateway. Their footsteps thundered on the bridge and they began to shout as the two great doors were closed and barred behind them.

Norman walked over to his uncle. 'We are ready now.' They smiled grimly at each other.

High up in the inner wall a window opened. A grey head was thrust out; a thin voice, not alarmed, but sleepy and irritable, called down into the quadrangle, 'What means that noise?'

Everyone looked up. David was amazed. This small, unimpressive man was the Cardinal. Then his mind became empty, and his body acted alone. The men's grip had relaxed. He wrenched himself free and ran towards the window.

'My lord, look to yourself! Norman Leslie has taken your castle!'

Once more there were shouts and footsteps behind him. A violent blow sent streaks of fire through his head. The gilded case was jerked out of his arms and the clasps flew open. David cried out as the crystal goblet somersaulted in the air, then splintered on the cobbles.

The two men dragged him up a winding stone stair. He was hustled along a corridor and through a doorway. One of the men kicked his shin. As he sprawled on his stomach he heard them lock the door.

For a long time he lay on the bare boards, too sick and giddy to move. When he sat up he had to fight the nausea that rose with every stroke of the bell throbbing outside.

He was in the Castle chapel. There were candles alight on the altar and incense was burning in a silver bowl beside it. An illuminated missal lay open on the Cardinal's *prie-dieu.*

David pulled himself to his feet and staggered to the windows that overlooked the front of the Castle. The foretower cut off his view on one side and the curve of the unfinished blockhouse on the other. In the small area he could see below the window, part of a large, roaring crowd seethed to and fro. There were more people pouring down Castle Wynd towards him, carrying poles and pikes and garden rakes and ladders. Despite the noise, they seemed frightened. As an arquebus shot exploded from the ramparts they stampeded out of sight. In a few moments they came back. David heard the clop of horses' hooves, and some orders were shouted, as if someone in authority had arrived. David pressed his aching head against the glass, but he could not see past the great square bulk of the foretower.

There were voices in the passage outside the chapel. David rushed to the locked door and beat on it with both fists. The men outside took no notice. They went by with shuffling footsteps and muffled bumps, as if they were dragging something heavy along the corridor. The sounds died away and David returned to the window that overlooked the forecourt.

Now the crowd was staring up at the blockhouse to his left. Even the children were quite still, all looking upwards. By twisting his neck David could see the top course of stones and the scaffolding round the unfinished wall. He saw moving feet and a large, shapeless bundle in a sheet, that was being heaved on to the wooden platform. A mason's trowel was kicked off the ledge and clattered into the forecourt. But the upturned faces did not move.

David saw Norman Leslie jump on to a projecting stone, swinging by one hand from the scaffolding. He waved the other mockingly at the crowd. Loud and exultant, his voice rang out:

'There, there, is your god!'

He sprang back on the wall and disappeared. The people below stirred; a low, shuddering sound came from their throats.

A sheet-corner dropped down the side of the blockhouse. It was stained with dark, wet patches. Then came a hand, loaded with rings, dabbled with blood, dangling at the end of a bare arm.

David jerked back from the window, although the clawed, swinging fingers were at least twenty feet away. The sheet caught against the wall, and then dropped lower. With it, suspended by one leg and the other arm, came a half-naked body. The head bobbed grotesquely on its gashed neck; the mouth gaped in a silent scream. It was the Cardinal.

CHAPTER THREE

The Quarrel

HE had been sick three times when the men came at noon to take him from the chapel. The town clock struck as they came in.

He had heard the advancing tide beat on the rocks as the angry, human voices died away. *'They've murdered the Cardinal, and I helped to let them in.'* He did not know whether the blow on his head or his own thoughts made him sick.

The two men were laughing as they unlocked the door.

'All right, laddie. Come with us.'

David drew his sword and sprang on guard with his dagger clenched in his left hand. He was too dizzy to fight well, but he was not afraid.

One of the men brushed the dagger aside. 'We mean no harm,' he said good-humouredly. But they gripped him firmly.

'Where are you taking me?' he shouted.

They pushed him down the winding stair and across the inner courtyard to the north wing of the Castle. It was humiliating to be treated like a boisterous calf, so he stopped struggling, and they led him to a room on the first floor.

'Bide there till your cousin comes!' they said, pushing him through the doorway. He heard them lock him in.

The room had belonged to one of the Cardinal's officials. There was arras on the walls and the tumbled bedclothes were of linen and damask. A crimson doublet and gown lay across an open chest, and above the bed hung a crucifix mounted in gold.

David flung himself on the disordered bed, with his hands pressed to his throbbing forehead. He saw wine on the table by the bed, and poured some out. He held the heavy, embossed goblet in both hands, and his teeth chattered against its silver rim. Gradually, as he drank, his hands stopped shaking.

As the shock of fear passed he became angry.

Why had he not had the wit to fight his way out to the town? And what right had the two Leslies to keep him prisoner? But most of all, he was angry with the bad luck that had ruined all his hopes and ambitions. There would be no honours for him now, no journey to Italy. It would be months before the new Archbishop began to think of such things. And whoever he was he would have no interest in David Lindsay.

David cursed and beat his fist on the table, making the empty wine-flagon totter.

How unfair it all was! To arrive in the middle of an assassination! For a moment he stopped thinking of his own misfortune. It was not only murder. It was sacrilege to kill a cardinal. The whole country would be excommunicated until the murderers atoned. And his father had said that Scotland would be quiet this year.

David stared dejectedly into the lees of his wine. What would his father have said, if he had seen the Cardinal dangling like butcher's meat from the tower? He had left Scotland twenty years ago, but his heart was still in this violent, divided country. Every evening he used to talk about the brave sword fights and neighbourly quarrels that spiced the dull days at Pitcairnie. He told stories about his grandfather, who had died at Flodden, and though he was now a wealthy, respectable merchant, he was proud of the unruly Scots nobles that no king could keep in order.

Staring at the heavy silver goblet, David remembered another, made of fragile Venetian glass. Scotland was a barbarous land. He thanked the saints that he had been born and bred in France. Once out of the Castle he would make the master of the *Giroflée* sail at once. His father would pay for the losses on the return cargo.

David put his head out of the window. The Castle wall fell sheer to a tangle of salty pools, and long, barnacled reefs. Beyond St Andrews Bay the Highland hills were a darker line of blue between the sea and the sky. The whole scene throbbed with heat.

Across the empty bay sailed a fleet of thirteen ships. Every sail was unfurled to the light breeze, as they tacked across the water in a slow, crab-like flight. And well in front of the others sailed the *Giroflée*. The ships had not stayed to unload their cargoes.

For a moment David would not believe it. When the sails had dwindled to tiny white specks, he had to accept the truth. The *Giroflée* had abandoned him. He was alone with a band of assassins, and he might never see Bordeaux and his family again.

Tears of despair and self-pity rushed to his eyes. The *Giroflée* had all his baggage: a dozen lawn shirts embroidered in black and gold, three velvet doublets and hose, two gold-laced hawking gloves with a set of jesses. And all his books. He put his head on the window-ledge and wept.

Afterwards, he went to the door and kicked and shouted. There were no sounds from the Castle. He could hear only the swish of waves below and the screeching gulls. Perhaps the murderers had run away. The Castle would be burnt to purge the terrible sin committed inside it and no one would know that he was there.

Hours later, when the light had begun to fade, a key grated in the lock. David swung round with his hand on his rapier. Martin came in.

He had exchanged his student's gown for a leather jerkin, and a dagger was buckled round his waist. He stood by the door and twisted his hands in his belt.

'Norman's sent me to bring you to supper.'

David stared, dumbfounded. The brutal events of the day had closed his mind to an obvious fact. Martin must have known about Leslie's plot.

'Hell have him and his supper! Tell him I must find a ship for France. Why am I locked in here?'

'You tried to warn the Cardinal.' Martin fidgeted unhappily with his dagger. 'Norman wants you to join us, David. Twenty Fife gentlemen rode in this afternoon. There'll be more tomorrow. Your cousin Pitcairnie's coming. The good news spreads fast.'

'Join you?' The pain of what he had only now realized made David feel sick again. He could not look at Martin as he asked, 'Did *you* know they meant murder?'

'No,' said Martin, and he looked regretful. 'I telt you, I thought it was about the English Testament. When I met them in the Priory Kirkyard, Norman sent me to the stables about his horse. He telt me to come back at nine. It was all over then.'

David grasped his friend's hand in relief. 'Martin, let's leave them. We'll stay at the Priory till there's a ship for France. You mustn't stay in Scotland now. My father will find you work in Bordeaux.'

Martin shook off his hand. 'I'm standing by Norman,' he said curtly. 'The Cardinal was a godless tyrant. He burnt George Wishart and many other poor souls. He deserved to die. His fat priests are like leeches on the body of Scotland. It was God's work that was done this morning, David.'

'Bonny work, indeed! Even in Bordeaux we knew that Leslie and his friends are in the pay of the English king. King Henry tried to have the Cardinal killed before. He knows that the French party will never give him Mary Stewart for his son. *That's* why the Cardinal was murdered, Martin.'

'He deserved to die,' repeated Martin obstinately. 'It is lawful to kill tyrants. Why should he keep God's word from us? His bishops never preach, but they make us pay for their masses.'

David cut him short with a jeer. 'How long do you think you can hold out here? The Regent will bring his guns from Edinburgh and the Queen Dowager will have a fleet from her brothers in France. In three months you will all be –'

He had been about to say, 'You will all be broken on the wheel,' but his throat tightened as he thought of it happening to Martin.

'King Henry will send provisions by sea. Norman has planned it all. The Regent canna raise an army till Parliament has met. Bide with us, David. We are doing the work of God!'

They had argued often before, but it had always been an intellectual game. Not like this, thought David in a panic, as he saw Martin's fanatical look. How could he believe that treason and assassination were the work of God? Not that the Cardinal had done the work of God, either, from what one heard. Anyway, what did the words mean? He tried to explain.

'Martin, I don't *want* to stay here. I must go back to France. Take me to the gates.'

'Norman has ordered them shut.'

'Ask him to open them.'

Martin frowned. 'He'd be angry. No.'

David sneered. 'So Norman is your hero, now? A fine Brutus he makes! Are you afraid to stay here without me? You always were a coward, Martin.'

Martin went pale and his voice became stiff and self-righteous. 'I'm not brave, but I ken what's right. You're as light as straw, David. D'you mind on our College disputations? You'd speak like Cicero for one side of the question, and when we'd all clapped you, you'd argue the other way, just to show off your fine wit. It was all a game. Nothing's serious for you—except maybe your clothes, and your light heathen books. You popinjay! A pity you werena born a lassie.'

David was silent. No words could stop the quarrel now. Martin went relentlessly on.

'You were the only lad in our year that had the Greek. When you went home at Easter we begged you to bring us back a Greek Testament, and teach us to read it. And you brought a book of heathen fables about witches and devils, not fit for a Christian man to read!'

David stirred in protest. 'I didn't know you wanted it so badly.'

Martin glared. 'God's truth has reached England, and now it comes to Scotland. The priests canna hold us back now. Beaton kent it. The last thing he cried was, *"Fie, fie, all is gone!"*'

David crossed himself.

'Leave yon mummery, David. Think on Christ Jesus and the Holy Evangel.'

'Will you murder the Queen Dowager too?' asked David bleakly. 'And the little Queen as well? She is three years old, Martin – old enough to be a danger to you Lutherans.'

'Words, more words! You're rotten with your own conceit. You'll never ken what to do with your life.'

He threw the key on the bed. 'There. You canna leave the Castle. Come for supper in the hall. You'll get no food otherwise.'

The air still seemed to ring with their angry words when he had gone. David stretched his arms to the lintel of the open door, staring into the dark corridor. Nothing would make him join the murderers in the hall. When he had escaped from the Castle he would never speak to Martin again. He would never come back to St Andrews.

But his belly ached with hunger. Perhaps someone in the kitchens would give him food.

He groped his way down to the quadrangle. The sky was a deep, luminous blue. It would hardly darken before dawn. A few figures stood in silhouette on the ramparts. The courtyard itself was leaping with light.

Near the well was a great blazing pyre, and in it the Cardinal burned in his gold vestments. David shrank back in terror, then he saw that it was only a bolster stuffed inside the robes. A crowd of men were dancing arm-in-arm round the fire and other figures darted to and fro behind them, hurling books and clothes into the flames.

David looked up at the lighted windows of the hall. His hunger overwhelmed him as he imagined the meats and pastries inside. It would be easy to go in and take Norman Leslie's hand. Why not, he thought. Only his pride stopped him and fear of the siege. David licked his mouth, moist with his craving for food.

Then he remembered the postern-gate. It was on the north side of the Castle, above a flight of steps hewn into the cliff. Sometimes, when the harbour was dry, the boatmen used to bring provisions for the Castle there. He had seen them doing it the first time he came from France.

David went back up the stair and began to feel his way along the corridor. By the shouts and flickers of light ahead of him, he must be near the kitchens. His groping hands felt stone, woodwork, and stone again. He counted five doors.

He began to think he had missed the postern, when he saw a faint blue glow at the end of a passage on his left. As he reached the opening he gave a gasp of joy. He was looking through an iron grille in the postern.

He pulled off the chain and levered back the bolts. For a moment his hands pressed the latch and he breathed fast, not daring to try the lock. Disbelievingly, he pulled the door open. They had forgotten about the sea-postern.

He smelt salty water and seaweed. He was on a small platform at the top of the steps. They led down to darkness, to the long reefs of the bay. He could see a distant gleam of water and hear its murmur, far back from the Castle rock. The tide was on the ebb again. It would be easy to clamber along the foot of the cliffs to the harbour. He must be careful not to wrench his ankle in the dim light. There was no other danger.

As he trod on the narrow, slippery steps, he drew back. He would need both hands free for the journey. His sword might trip him. Unwillingly he took off his rapier. He rubbed the inlaid silver hilt; and quickly, before he could change his mind, whirled the sword round his head, and threw it towards the sea. Then he turned to face the rock, and lowered himself down the steps, one by one.

He was half-way down when lights flared on the rampart above him and he heard drunken shouts. One of the torches hurtled towards him, but it seemed thrown to light the steps rather than aimed to hit him. He crouched against the steps, inching his way down. There was a small burst of flame, an explosion, and a bullet chipped the step by his face. A piece of stone stung his cheek.

David began to hurry recklessly. In a few yards the bulge of the cliff would shelter him. If only one of them had a hand-gun, he would never reload in time to fire again.

He did not see the second burst of flame; he heard the explosion, and a red-hot pain ripped the side of his left foot. The drunken shouts were suddenly gone and the torchlight disappeared.

David slid a hand over his left foot. His fingers met a pulpy, unfeeling mass that was oozing stickily. He had to go on; he had to escape before the pain came and forced him to stop.

As he slithered and crawled round the base of the Castle rock, he remembered some unpleasant facts about gunshot wounds. They became poisoned immediately; they had to be cauterized with hot iron; and they often led to amputations.

He shuddered, and then gasped as he stepped into a pool of salt water. The injured foot began to throb and spasms of pain ran up his ankle. Again and again, as he climbed the rocks, he fell into pools left by the ebbing tide. He looked back at the Castle: the men had gone from the ramparts, but the fortress still loomed above him, frighteningly close.

At last he came to a path that ran obliquely towards the top of the cliffs. It was too near the Castle, but he knew that he could never reach the harbour now, climbing over the reefs and boulders. He had to drag himself up the path on one leg; still, the steep rise was easier to manage than the slippery clumps of seaweed by the cliffs.

When David reached level ground he realized how badly he was hurt. His left leg was stiff and ached from foot to thigh. He had to rest at every other step, and the sea water ran clammily down his legs.

There was noise and light in the Castle, but the town was silent. All the windows were shuttered; no lanterns had been put out on the forestairs, and even the pigs and cattle in the backyards seemed to have been frightened into dumbness.

David shuffled towards the house of Master Reid. In the darkness he stumbled over a pile of slates. The clatter might have roused the whole street; yet not a single window opened.

Every part of Master Reid's house was bolted: the bakery, the front door, and even the garden gate. David stumbled back down the forestair, after calling and knocking at the door. The pain in his foot was worse, and his head was swimming. He would go to the Priory. The canons had an infirmary where they could dress his wound. They had to give shelter to anyone who needed it. He muttered this to reassure himself, and he limped painfully to the Priory gatehouse.

The doors were closed, but a light burned in the porter's lodge above. He jangled the bell and leant against the postern gate. A closed lantern glowed dully behind the grille.

'What do you want?' said a cold voice.

'I've hurt my foot. Please let me in.'

The light disappeared for a moment. When it came back there was a mutter of two voices. A cowled head pressed against the grille. The dark, shadowed face watched him for a moment. Then the second voice said, 'We cannot admit you.'

'You must! It's against your rules to shut me out.'

The voice said, 'There are no rules now,' and a wooden shutter was slammed across the grille.

The pain was agonizing. It shot from his ankle to his knee and there turned into a hot flush that swept through his whole body. He did not know where he was, nor how long he had been in the empty streets. He clutched at one thought. He must get down to the harbour and find a ship for France.

By this time the house-walls were strangely lop-sided and spinning slowly from side to side. He was staggering towards a gleam of water, and he thought it must be the harbour. Then he tried to reach a small point of light ahead of him. It turned into a multitude of tiny points of brightness in the crevices of a rubble wall. He bumped into a hut that was piled, rather than built, against the gable-end of some large building on the quay. A larger band of light streamed above an unhinged door that was propped from inside the hut against the entrance.

He opened his mouth, but could make no sound. He sagged against the wood, and the door swung back a little.

'If you please,' he whispered, and felt himself falling. He crashed into the hut, lying on top of the door.

CHAPTER FOUR

Enter a Cousin

DAVID choked and fought for breath. Someone tugged the door beneath him and he rolled off. The figure put the door upright against the entrance.

It was the fisher-girl. There was an old woman with her, very stout and wrinkled, working at a fishing-net by the light of a single crusie-lamp. They both shrank back in terror.

David struggled to his elbows. The hut was stiflingly hot. A peat fire burned under a rough chimney built against the wall, and the lamp stank of rancid fish-oil. The straw thatch above seemed to be pressing down on his face.

'He's one of *them*,' said the girl.

The old woman blinked and peered. 'Poor laddie. He's sore hurt.'

The girl snapped, 'He'll bring us trouble. Master Reid says he went into the Castle with Norman Leslie.'

David groped for the strings of his purse. 'The men in the Castle shot me. Don't turn me out. I'll give you – I'll give you two of my father's rings. Look, they're gold.'

The girl took the rings in her hand. She looked sharply at David, and held the seals close to the lamp. She handed back the rings with an ironical smile. 'You're free and easy with your siller.' She seemed to have relented. 'Is he bad, then?'

The old woman squatted by David and her fingers moved shakily over his left ankle. 'Fetch me the wee leather bag. I'll say the words and put a red thread on him.'

'No! Father Anthony said you were never to do that again. Only clean water, he said.'

'Tchah!' The old woman pulled a sulky face, but she gave in. 'Where shall we put him, Elspeth?'

'Inby. I'll tell Master Reid in the morning.'

She stepped over two piles of heather that seemed to be their beds and pulled aside some sacking on the far wall. Behind it was a stone doorway with a carved lintel. She lit another crusie, and went through. When she returned the two women pulled and lifted David through the opening into a small warehouse, full of barrels and bales of straw. Elspeth tumbled down two of the bales and threw some fishing-nets across them.

'He'll never miss his fine linen tonight,' she said.

For a moment they left him alone. Then the girl whispered inside the hut, 'I'll not let you! It's your own supper.'

'Ach, I'm not wanting it. He needs a bite.'

The old woman came through with a bowl of greasy broth. David tilted the bowl and sucked greedily. The old woman watched him, her head bobbing from side to side. 'Elspeth!' she called.

The girl brought in a crock of hot water. The old woman plucked at the top of David's blue hose.

'They're sewn to his breeks!' she exclaimed.

'It's a court fashion,' said the girl scornfully. 'Take his dagger and cut them below the knee.'

The dagger was a duelling weapon, notched along the blade. The old woman's hands trembled and she could not cut the cloth.

'Here, let me. You'll leave him no flesh at all. You're not gutting a haddie.'

Swiftly she ripped his hose below the left knee and removed the cloth. David lifted his head to see the wound, and lay back with a sick groan.

'Yon's an awful sight,' whimpered the old woman.

'Wheesht,' said Elspeth. She pulled the crusie near and bent over David's foot. The impatient, suspicious look went from her face. She squeezed hot water over the clotted blood and dabbed at it cautiously. David cried out as she pulled away the matted pieces of cloth and leather.

After half an hour she sighed and sat back on her heels. 'That's all I can do. I hope I didna hurt you. Father Anthony will have to use his instruments.'

The old woman went back to the hut. For a moment Elspeth stayed behind, staring at David. 'I've seen you before. Before yesterday, I mean.'

'I was at St Leonard's last year,' said David faintly.

'What's your name? Master Reid never told me.'

'David Lindsay. From Bordeaux.' He wished she would go away and leave him to sleep.

'Lindsay. That's a good Fife name. My mother was a Lindsay.'

She took the crusie away with her.

David lay in the darkness, his eyes wide open with horror. This ragged, dirty girl his cousin? It was impossible! He laughed. The wound had shocked him out of his senses. Lindsay was a common name in Fife, and there was no sign of his aunt, who would be no more than middle-aged ... He tossed a few times in the prickly straw to ease his aching foot, and soon fell asleep.

He woke in a glare of sunlight that was streaming through a small window high in the wall. The heat brought out the warehouse smells: pickled fish, tanned hides, and the scaly odour of the nets beneath him. He was very stiff and his foot throbbed fiercely.

David looked in dismay at his clothes. His hose were tattered below the knee and his doublet was stained with sea water. He would have to visit a tailor before he left the town.

The thought made him reach out for his purse. It had disappeared. He sat up and rummaged under the nets. He could not find it and he glared at the sacking hung over the doorway. Did the old woman and girl think they could rob him because he could not walk?

As he opened his mouth for an angry shout, there was a squeak and rustle beside him. The noise came from the red-crested monkey, squatting on a barrel. It was swinging his purse between its paws and nibbling at the gold tassels.

David lay back with a grin and snapped his fingers. The monkey shambled nearer, but when he stretched to take the purse, it bounded away with an angry squeal.

Elspeth brought in some barley bread and water. 'We've no broth this morning,' she said gruffly.

David felt a small pang of shame for his suspicions. 'Your monkey's taken my purse.'

Elspeth leapt across the narrow room. 'Mahound!' she shrieked. 'Put yon down!'

The monkey gibbered and bounced to and fro. At last Elspeth managed to seize the purse, and gave it back to David. She patted the monkey on the head. 'Never mind, my honey, we'll find you another bauble. Leave the laddie in peace now.'

'I must have a surgeon,' said David. 'My foot's poisoned.'

'I'll fetch you Father Anthony when he comes back from the lepers at St Nicholas. He's the infirmary father at the Priory.'

David frowned. He had known some of the Priory canons, but this was a new name. 'Will he be out? The Priory gate was locked last night.'

She said hotly, 'He goes to them every morning. Nothing would stop him. I'll bring him when I've done my fishing.'

David eyed her curiously. She was about the same age as his twin sisters. Even in their fine gowns and furs, she would have looked a strange, uncouth creature. He thought of the modest eyes and soft giggles of the girls he knew in Bordeaux.

'Do you like fishing?'

Elspeth's mouth widened in fierce amusement. She would have been pretty, David decided, if her black hair had not been so tangled.

'Aye, when the weather's good.'

'It's strange work for a girl.'

'Who else would do it?'

An unappeased doubt nagged him. 'Where's your family?'

A defensive look came over her face. 'My father drowned last spring. There's none of his folk alive, except my grandmother.'

'Where's your mother?'

Elspeth dropped her eyes. 'She died of the plague eight years past. She didna belong to St Andrews. She came from near the Lomonds, a place called Pitcairnie.'

Her face hardened as if she regretted telling him. 'Is there any more you'd like to ken?' she asked roughly. She hurried through the door, saying, 'Hold tight to your pouch. Mahound's a thieving beast.'

David forgot the pain in his leg. So it was true. She was his cousin. He was kin to the women in this filthy hovel. He scowled with disgust that this outrageous thing had been added to his other misfortunes. They must never find out. They were beggars too, most likely; they would plague him for money if they knew.

As the morning crept on, and his wound ached more and more painfully, David began to stream with sweat. He lifted his leg to ease it, biting his tongue so that he would not cry out. How much longer would the priest be? Had Elspeth told him that he could afford to keep his altar in wax candles for a month?

The old woman crooned to herself next door, but she did not visit him. Later he heard her talking to someone. A man's voice said, 'You will have to make up the fire.'

A coil of fear twisted in David's stomach. He had tried to forget what happened to gunshot wounds. The surgeon seared the flesh and filled the wound with boiling oil of elders. David's throat went dry.

He heard the rustle of the priest's robes as Father Anthony pushed open the sacking curtain. He was a bulky, tall man, about forty-five years old. He looked almost bald, for his tonsured hair was white. Out of the pale smooth face looked very deep brown eyes. He smiled and dropped on his knees to examine David's foot.

'I'm sorry to see this.'

David swallowed. 'I'll be grateful for your help, Father.'

The canon unpacked his case of instruments and picked out a slender metal probe.

'I'll try not to hurt you, but I must look for the ball. Was it an arquebus shot?'

'Yes – oh!' David cried out, and then stuffed his hand in his mouth, in case the women heard him. He tried not to wince or move as the last pieces of cloth and leather were removed.

'You're lucky,' said the canon at last. 'The shot didn't lodge in your foot.'

'Good,' said David, in a tight whisper. The worst was still to come.

Father Anthony called through the doorway, 'Now, Mistress Binnie, please!'

The old woman brought in two earthenware bowls. One held hot water and in the other was an egg. After cleaning the wound, Father Anthony broke the egg into the bowl and poured some thick oils on top. As he beat the mixture, David watched in astonished fear. In a shaking voice, he asked, 'Do you want me next door for the cautery?'

The canon looked up. 'Did you think I'd use a hot iron on your foot?'

'It is usual, isn't it?'

The canon touched his hand. 'Your foot will heal better without being burnt.'

'Gunpowder is poison,' argued David. 'Surgeons always burn a gunshot wound.'

'I learnt my surgery in France, with Ambrose Paré. He taught me to use oil of roses and turpentine instead of a hot iron. I promise you, your wound will not become poisoned.' He smiled at David's relieved but incredulous face.

He laid the mixture on the wound and bandaged it with clean linen. 'There. I'll come back tomorrow to clean and dress it again. You won't be able to walk on your foot for two or three weeks, and it'll be longer before you can walk in comfort.'

David sat up eagerly. 'Father, can I lodge at the Priory? I can pay well. I'll make an offering at your altar as well.'

The canon packed away his instruments and bottles of salves. 'My altar is dedicated to Saint Cosmas and Saint Damian, Master David. I accept only what will pay for its upkeep. Give your money to the Priory almoner, if you wish. But I'm afraid the sub-Prior won't receive any strangers now.'

'You can't think I'm one of Leslie's men! You dressed my wound.'

'I would have dressed it anyway . . . I'm sorry, our guest-rooms are full. The Cardinal's household have come to us. They have filled all the inns in the town as well.'

'Where can I say till my foot is healed?' cried David, looking round the warehouse.

'You might let these good people look after you, if they're willing. They've already put themselves to great trouble.' The canon's voice was edged.

David flushed. 'I'll pay them well when I leave.'

'No doubt,' said the canon drily.

Then he smiled. 'You were at St Leonard's, weren't you? So was I. There's something I can do for you. Would you like to write a letter to your family? There will be messengers going from here to the Regent, and it will be easy to find a ship for France in Leith harbour. I'll bring you pen and paper tomorrow.'

He went into the hut to talk to Mistress Binnie. David heard the old woman repeat some instructions, and after that she began to complain about the men in the Castle. Her voice became shrill.

'The lairds and gentry never did us townsfolk any good. Why canna they leave poor bodies alone? Murdering, upland loons! May they burn at the stake, and roast in hell!'

The canon replied sternly, 'Janet Binnie, stop your curses. Hasn't there been enough murder? Pray for the Cardinal's soul and for those misguided men in the Castle, too.'

David drowsed on the straw bales for the rest of the morning. As the heat began to stifle him, he pulled off his velvet doublet, and after it, the gold-embroidered shirt. The sweat still trickled down his back legs. Two or three weeks, the canon had said. Three weeks in this pigsty with the old crone and the fisher-girl! He would have done better to stay with Martin.

He tossed on the straw. The thought of Martin was a bitter, angry pain; he tried to drive him from his mind. He moved clumsily on one leg round the warehouse. It was larger than the hut, soundly built, but the window was too high for him, and the double doors opening on the quay were barred outside.

At midday the old woman brought him some broth. 'Elspeth's away to cook Master Reid's dinner,' she mumbled.

David wiped his damp face on his shirtsleeve and grinned in sudden relief. What a fool he had been! He could stay with Master Reid. The girl could take a message for him. He would lodge with the merchant until a French ship came into port.

In the afternoon he hacked off the tatters of his lower hose with his dagger. He studied Father Anthony's bandage with admiration, thankful to feel the pain of his wound soothed away. In a more cheerful mood he waited for Elspeth.

She came home in the early evening looking very hot and tired. Her sunburnt face glistened with sweat, and she sat down beside him without speaking. She was breathing fast and seemed angry. Later, David realized that she was frightened.

'There's more of them ridden into the Castle,' she began abruptly. 'From all over Fife, Master Reid said.'

'What's happened in the town?'

'It's like a dead place. The kirk bells aren't ringing.

There's to be no more mass. Folk are peering through the shutters, like when the plague came from Dundee.'

David shuddered.

'Master Reid said he saw six of them steal some cows when the town herdsman drove them out this forenoon. Nobody went to help him! It'll be weeks before the Regent can start the siege.'

David mopped irritably at his perspiring face. 'Why can't the Sheriff of Fife begin it?'

'You're an ignorant loon! Our sheriff is Norman Leslie. Master Reid says half the gentry of Fife are behind him.' Her voice became whining and broken, very like the old woman's. 'I'm feared. I wish I didna have to go past the Castle gates to get to Master Reid's.'

'Stay at home, then,' said David uneasily.

'How would we eat? I canna make enough by the fishing. Forbye, he has a claim on me. He gave me the price of my boat.'

David began to give her his message for Master Reid. His cheeks were hot as he remembered the canon's rebuke, and he tried not to hurt the girl's feelings. She cut short his careful excuses.

'Lodge with him – he'd never let you inby the house! He says you came from France to join Norman Leslie.'

'What!' cried David in a rage. 'He knows well I didn't.'

'Maybe, but the Town Council might not think so.' She looked sideways at David. 'He says we're daft to keep you here.'

He was too absorbed in his anger against the merchant to realize that Elspeth was waiting for a word of thanks. He did not notice her tiny shrug, either, as if she had put the hope aside.

She held up a bundle wrapped in a white napkin, and

grinned. 'He'd not eat what I cooked for him. Look—a hare-pie, all free, and on top of my wages. We'll have it for supper.'

'Is it burnt?' asked David cautiously.

'No! He's off his meat since the *Giroflée* took all his gear back to France. He says he's ruined. The Deacon of the Bakers winna let him fire his ovens again because he left the craft to become a merchant. Still, it's lucky for you. You can stay in his warehouse as long as you like.'

David looked discontentedly at his foot. 'What can I do all day long?'

Elspeth was surprised. 'Why should you weary? Folk like you dinna work.'

'I work very hard! I read Greek and Latin. I study logic, mathematics and astronomy. I can write sonnets in Italian.' He decided to crush her. 'At Bordeaux I spend an hour every day in the fencing school. And I can play and sing my own music for the lute.' His voice faltered. Master Reid had his lute. No doubt he would make a fine profit by selling it when the court came to St Andrews.

Elspeth seemed more puzzled than impressed. 'D'you want something to read, then?' She picked up a sheaf of papers from a barrel and handed them to him upside-down.

David rustled through them contemptuously. 'These are only old bills of lading.'

Elspeth peered over his shoulder at the customs clerk's minutely scrawled lists. 'I canna read.'

David jabbed a scornful finger. '"Item. Three lasts of salted salmon. Item. Ten dozen coney skins –"' He broke off as he saw Elspeth's downcast face. 'I suppose it's better than nothing,' he said ungraciously.

'A pity you dinna have to fish for your books! Three hours I was out in the bay this forenoon, and I got only one wee codling. I went out again after dinner, when I should have been mending the nets. I got this blister. Look!'

David stared down at her raw hand. 'Did you go out twice because of me?'

'Aye,' she muttered sulkily. 'My grandmother wants you here, and you cause me more work than a dozen bairns.'

'I'm sorry, Elspeth. I'd go fishing for you if I could walk to the boat.'

Her face cleared at once. 'Maybe you could do the nets instead.'

David wondered if she was laughing at him. 'All right. Show me.'

'It's hard. It's not just the knot. You have to keep the meshes even.'

'I'll try.'

She smiled at him. 'Not in those braw clothes.'

David shrugged. 'The hose are in tatters, and I never wear an unmatched doublet. Anyway, they're too hot. If only I could get down to the sea!'

'Wait.' Elspeth went into the hut. She came back with a wooden bucket full of water and a bundle of linen.

'Tip the water over you and put these on. My father used to wear them in summer.' She added defensively, 'They're clean.'

When she left him, David stripped off the remnants of his hose and breeches, and gulped down some of the brackish water. He supported himself against the wall and sluiced the dirt and sweat from his body. He rubbed himself dry with handfuls of straw.

With a grimace he put on the fisherman's clothes. There were loose breeches and a jerkin of coarse, unbleached linen. They were clean, as Elspeth had promised, and smelt of dried rosemary.

Elspeth called through the sacking, 'Are you ready?' and put her head through. She stared; then threw back her head and laughed. Not the polite titter of the Bordeaux girls, but a raucous boy's laugh, that twisted her thin body, and screwed up her face and eyes.

'You make a fine fisher-laddie. But your skin's as white as a lady's!'

She helped him into the hut. The old woman was cutting up the hare-pie, and the monkey was munching two green apples on top of a wooden chest.

'It's a feast we have tonight,' cried Mistress Binnie. 'Even Mahound has done well for himself. Eh, my moppet?' She shook her knife at him.

'He goes over the Priory wall,' said Elspeth, 'and steals from the canons' orchard.'

'What for not?' cackled the old woman. 'The Kirk takes a tithe of all we have.'

Elspeth looked frightened. 'Wheesht! Yon's an unchancy thing to say.'

The old woman handed David a slice of the pie. 'Nobody thinks I'm friends with those murdering loons in the Castle.'

Elspeth's face relaxed as she took her own share of the pie. She licked her lips greedily. 'After supper we'll sit on the quay and I'll show you how we do the nets.' She waited for David to eat a few mouthfuls before she began herself.

'There,' she said triumphantly. 'It's not burnt, is it?'

CHAPTER FIVE

The Harbour

THE next morning David sat outside the hut and tried to knot the thin cord as Elspeth had shown him. He could not stand up to hang the net from the hooks bedded for it in the thatch; he had to work on his knee.

After half an hour his hands felt as if they had been rubbed raw. It had looked so simple when Elspeth showed him. His fingers slipped clumsily on the knots, and he had little to show for six hours' work. Yet something drove him on.

He hid his dagger under some bales of straw, but strapped the purse to his waist, so that he would be ready if a French ship came into the harbour. He pulled off the golden tassels and gave them to Mahound, who dozed beside him in the sun.

All day the fierce sun beat down on the quay. By late afternoon his bare arms and legs were scorched red.

In the morning the fishermen walked down the hill in twos and threes. They ignored him, full of their own anxieties. The tide lifted their small, undecked boats off the mud, but the fishermen stayed all day at the quayside, arguing and shouting. They huddled into pugnacious groups whenever a new figure appeared. They seemed afraid to sail out to the bay: they had left their families in the town – too near the Castle. They had come down to guard their boats. At sunset they began to straggle up Kirk Hill again, to their homes in the Fishergate.

When Elspeth had tied her skiff to the harbour wall and climbed the ladder, she inspected David's work.

'What's yon meant to catch? A whale?'

He winced at her outspokenness. After dinner he tried again. It had been the same at Gaston's fencing-school. 'No, no, Monsieur David! Your dagger held *so*. *Mon Dieu,* what clumsy hands! You will never fence like a Frenchman!'

Once, furtively, he had tried to carve a block of wood. The snarling lion's head he had imagined remained a shapeless lump. He had thrown the wood back into the log-basket.

After long practice he could now fence and play the lute. But his hands were still slow to learn.

Hour after hour he went on with the monotonous knotting of the twine. On the third day, after Elspeth returned from the town, he held up his net and waited for her usual sharp comment.

She nodded briskly. 'Aye, that's better. They might catch some fish in that.'

David grinned. He felt extraordinarily pleased.

Elspeth had not caught many fish herself that day. She blamed the bright, glaring sunlight in the bay.

'When I can walk,' said David, 'I'll take the boat out for you at night. Perhaps they'd bite better in the dark.' He took some coins hesitatingly from his purse. He had not forgotten what happened the last time he offered Elspeth money. 'Why not buy some food in the market? Some meat – maybe some wine.' He thought of the pastries and sweetmeats that came out of his mother's kitchen.

Elspeth pushed the money away. 'There's no food to buy. The country-folk'll not bring it to market, and the townsfolk are keeping theirs hidden. They're all feared of Norman Leslie's men. Did you hear the fishermen? They said the Cardinal's blood will drive the fish out of the bay. What nonsense!'

David's skin prickled. Who knew what strange events might follow a sacrilegious murder? Meteors and comets shot through the sky when a great man died. Elspeth, in her uneducated ignorance, had spoken rashly.

'My father says the herring were leaving this coast when he was a boy at Pitcairnie. Maybe your line-fish are moving away, too.' He tried to show her what a world of knowledge she had missed. 'The fish, like ourselves, may be governed by the stars. Perhaps the influence of the planets extends to the ocean. The moon –'

Elspeth interrupted with a rude laugh. 'The moon! And maybe the fairies have taken the fish out of the sea! What nonsense you collegers talk. You blether like my grandmother, David.' She pushed a basket of mussels towards him. 'I'm going out again this afternoon. Here, help me bait these hooks.'

After a fortnight his fingers were as hard and brown as Elspeth's, and his skin had darkened to the colour of leather. He saw his reflection in a bucketful of water: his hair was bleached like new straw, and the face staring back at him was a Moor's.

He tried again to give Elspeth money, but once more she refused it. So he worked even harder at the nets, and sometimes became sullen, because he could not settle his debt.

During this time the townsfolk began to creep out of doors again. The Cardinal was dead and his body had disappeared; but they still had to bake their bread and give food to their children. A few fishermen went out to sea. David watched them sail out, one or two at first, and then the whole fleet, although they never moved out of sight of the harbour.

Elspeth brought him the news from the town. The

magistrates had sent angry messages to the country parishes, reminding them that it was illegal for the people to buy or sell among themselves, except in the burgh market, where the proper tolls could be levied. The countryfolk took no notice. They kept away and food became short in the town.

No more ships came into the harbour, not even the coasting vessels that brought the coal from south Fife. Mistress Binnie complained that the Priory was like a fortress now. The gates were always shut. There were no daily alms for the poor, and she missed her weekly basket of coals.

The Castilians (as people were calling them) were now one hundred and fifty strong. They walked round the town and exercised their horses on the common lands, where they soon trampled down the citizens' barley and beans. They drank and gambled in the ale-houses. The Cardinal's wine was better, but they seemed bored with their cramped quarters. The ale-house keepers listened in silence to their boasts, and when they saw them coming they sent their womenfolk to a neighbour's house.

Elspeth heard from Master Reid that the Regent's son had been in the Castle when Leslie took it. He had been living there as a pledge for his father's good behaviour. People said that the Regent wanted to make terms with the Castilians. He was secretly glad of the Cardinal's death. He had feared and hated the Cardinal, because he had made him break off the marriage treaty with England. Now he was using his son as an excuse to delay the siege. Parliament had not yet voted to raise an army.

Twice already, because of the cancelled treaty, King Henry had sent his soldiers into Scotland. They had brought the plague with them, and burned and plundered as far as the shores of Fife. The Scots called it the 'Rough Wooing'. Now the Castilians waited for the third invasion, confident that at last the Queen Dowager would have to hand over her daughter, and King Henry's army would march into St Andrews.

David listened wearily to all these reports. What did it matter whether young Mary Stewart married an English prince or a French dauphin? There would always be fighting, and famine, and disease in Scotland. The ordinary people would survive somehow, while the quarrelsome nobles found another excuse to fight each other.

He kept his eyes fixed on the bay. If only a French ship would come! 'Holy Mother, send me a ship and I will never try to go to Italy again. I'll become a wine-merchant and betroth myself to Marie, the daughter of my father's partner, as he wishes.'

No ship came.

Father Anthony called in every day, on his way to the lepers' hospital, to change the dressing on David's wound. He had told him not to walk on his foot until it was completely healed. David tried to prolong the canon's visits. The old woman was poor company for him. For long hours she would go into some private world, muttering and chuckling to herself.

In this way he learnt that Father Anthony had once been a soldier. The canon had been talking about the Priory herb garden, where he grew most of his remedies.

'I sometimes use mercury or theriac as well. Only a little. The apothecaries prescribe far too much. Simples are better. I don't agree with too much blood-letting, either. I tell my patients I can't bleed them now I am a priest.' He smiled. 'Not strictly true. Prior Wynram gives me an indulgence to use my surgeon's knife if it's needed.' He saw David staring at his broad shoulders and arms, and laughed.

'Did you think I was born in these black robes? I've been a priest for five years. I studied medicine at Montpellier. Then I was a surgeon in the French army.' His face darkened. 'That's where I learnt my surgery, not in the schools. At the siege of Turin, with Ambroise Paré. He taught me all I know.'

David did not dare to ask what had turned him from a physician to a priest.

'I wanted to go to Italy, too,' he said.

Father Anthony was silent for a moment. Then he said, 'After that, I went to Paris to study some more anatomy. I worked in the Maison Dieu Hospital. It was there I decided to become a priest.'

'I see,' said David, but he did not see at all. How could a man take such an enormous decision? And if one hadn't the courage to decide, would one always be tossed by the violence of other men's lives? Misery and homesickness overwhelmed him. He blurted out, 'Was it easy?'

Father Anthony's brown eyes watched him steadily. 'No. But it was simple.'

David remembered Martin's fanatical look as he said, 'The last thing he cried was, "Fie, fie, all is gone!"' Martin, too, had been sure of what he wanted.

'But it must be easy, if you always know the right thing to do.' He looked at the canon boldly. 'You have always known your own mind, Father.'

'No. I have often had to act in doubt. Sometimes you can't wait to be sure. You must choose and hope you have chosen well. When I was at Turin I had to sit up with some wounded men, the night after we took the city. A soldier came in with a cocked pistol – one of those new wheel-locks, have you seen them? He said he would kill me. He thought he was still fighting, but he was drunk and wild with rage. I hadn't time to call for help. I told myself that if *I* died, all my patients would die too. We hadn't enough physicians to look after them.'

'What did you do?'

Father Anthony's long mouth drew in. 'I used one of my surgeon's knives to kill him.' He dropped his eyes. 'Afterwards, I was ashamed. I wondered if I had really wanted to save my own life, not my patients. Besides, I know now that I couldn't be sure they'd die without me. I must wait for God's judgement.'

David sighed. 'At least you had something to guide you.'

'What will you do when you return to Bordeaux?'

David shook his head. A few weeks ago he would have talked of the Italian courts, the libraries, and the pretty women. Now he did not know. 'My hands,' he said, before he knew he had said the words. 'I wish I could use my hands. To carve, or paint, or work in silver. It's a stupid thought. I have no skill, and it would be unsuitable for me to become a craftsman's apprentice.' He picked up the meshing-pin and ball of twine. 'Well, there are always Elspeth's nets to mend,' he laughed.

The canon nodded, but seemed to check his first reply. 'I mustn't hold you from your work,' he said instead. 'And I must go to the lepers. I'm not allowed to say mass with them now, but I think it helps them if I go.'

Elspeth no longer brought back food from Master Reid's house, and the hens in the town stopped laying.

'It's the Cardinal's blood,' said Mistress Binnie. 'The corn will be blighted and there will be no fruit in the Priory orchard. I'll have to try the fishermen.'

David saw Elspeth seize her grandmother's arm. 'You promised the canon not to!'

The old woman shook her off with a sly look. 'The priests dinna say mass for us now. We'll try the other way.'

During the next few days some fine crabs and whiting appeared outside the hut. Elspeth cooked them, but her face was grim as she bent over the pot, and she snapped at both David and her grandmother.

David saw how the fishermen stepped aside when the old woman passed them on the quay. Some of them crossed themselves, or closed one finger and thumb together in a curious way.

One morning a fisherman brought a net to be mended. He dropped it by the door and called to Elspeth. While he waited for an answer, he kept his eyes turned over his shoulder. When the old woman came out he stepped back so quickly that he tripped over a lobster-pot. Mistress Binnie walked past him without noticing.

Elspeth stared back defiantly at David's surprised look.

'It's gey unlucky to meet a woman on the way to the boat, they think.' She laughed uneasily.

'He isn't going out today. He just said so.'

Her eyes wavered and she shook the net fiercely, looking for the broken meshes. 'All right, then. You can see for yourself. They dinna like us. They're feared of my grandmother.'

He held the other end of the net for her. 'Why do they bring the nets to you? Couldn't their own women mend them?'

'They want to help us ... My father was a cadger. He had his own pack-train, but the beasts all died in the plague. So he bought a fishing-boat. He took some of them on. They were glad of the work.' Her voice began to shake. 'That was eight years syne. Last spring – that man was on my father's boat when he drowned off the Isle of May. It was a terrible storm. The others nearly drowned with him. We couldna pay the rent in the Fishergate, after my father – well, we came down here. The fishermen built the hut for us.' She turned her face away.

'Elspeth,' said David gently, 'what happened to the boat?'

'When they got back, they burnt it. The keel's on the shore near the lepers' hospital.'

'*Burnt* it?'

'They said it was unlucky. They think they'll catch my father's luck if they stand too near us. Fisherfolk have queer notions, David. Still, they dinna want us to starve. They bring us their nets.'

'Is that all? When they have taken your living from you?'

Elspeth shrugged. 'What way could we use a fishing-boat? We have no men in the family.'

'I shall tell her,' thought David. 'Perhaps it'll help her.' He could accept her as his cousin now, without disgust. Yet when he opened his mouth the words would not come. Some day he would be able to tell her. Perhaps when he was leaving St Andrews. Not yet.

He lay awake that night, tormented by a deep unhappiness he could not understand. When he slept, his dreams were full of storms and men with enormous hands who tried to pull him into the sea.

He could make no sense of his dreams; but he knew they had started with the thought that the fishermen had set fire to the boat that should have belonged to Elspeth.

CHAPTER SIX

A Basket of Eels

'Your wound has healed well,' said Father Anthony. He flexed David's toes up and down. 'You mustn't walk too far at first.'

David looked with satisfaction at his brown feet. The wound had been unbandaged for a long time now, and all that showed was a puckered white scar running from his middle toe to his instep.

'I'll be able to walk to the gangplank of the next ship for France.'

'No ship will call here now.'

'Then I'll buy a horse in the town.'

'Even that will be difficult. You aren't fit to ride yet. I'll bring you something to read while you wait.'

David wondered if he would see Martin when he walked up to the town. The thought of his friend still hurt him. Had he been named among the outlaws? Elspeth said the Castilians had jeered when a herald read the summons of treason in front of the Castle walls. The next day they moved round the streets as freely as ever.

David opened the book eagerly when the canon brought it. Inside the leather covers he found only manuscript notes and sketches. He stammered his thanks and wondered resentfully why the canon had not brought him a printed book from the Priory library.

'These are my medical notes,' said the canon, apparently not noticing David's disappointment. 'Some of the sketches are very rough. At Montpellier we used to pay the hangman to let us dissect corpses. It was illegal, so I was in a hurry. The better ones I did under Ambroise Paré. The French physicians despise him, because he performs his own operations, and is only a barber-surgeon. He knows more anatomy than anyone except Vesalius of Padua. He's the finest surgeon in Europe. He rebuked me for writing my notes in Latin.' The canon smiled. 'That's my only disagreement with him.'

David was impressed. 'Thank you. I'll handle the book carefully.' He would glance at the notes to please Father Anthony. At least it would pass the time.

After supper, he took a crusie-lamp as usual into the warehouse. He heard Elspeth and the old woman turning on their heather beds; the old woman's snores mingled with the gurgle of the burn running into the harbour.

David yawned. The Latin notes were technical and full of abbreviations. He struggled with them for a few moments before he turned to the diagrams. David exclaimed in delight at the pen-and-ink sketches. The canon was a fine draughtsman.

Then his mouth curved in distaste at the subjects: disjointed legs and arms, the skin peeled back to show the braided muscles; tendons and sinews looped round the bones like slack bowstrings. It was repellent to see human flesh sliced away and the organs displayed like parts of a clock.

Yet he could not put the book aside. His horror lessened and the diagrams began to fascinate him. He took off his canvas jerkin and doubled his fingers and forearm, trying to trace the muscles in the sketches. He had never thought before about what lay under the skin and hair. He prodded at the scar on his foot, amazed that such an intricate thing could heal so well.

At the end of the book he began again. This time he

deciphered the notes. He tried the Latin phrases on his tongue, entranced by his new knowledge.

When the flame of the crusie guttered and died in a terrible stench of fish-oil, David tried to read by moonlight. He peered until the moon climbed too high to throw its light through the window. Then, reluctantly, he climbed on his bales of straw.

Next morning Elspeth put her head through the curtain and asked why he was so late coming to breakfast.

David did not lift his eyes. 'I'm reading Father Anthony's book.'

She came to stand by his shoulder. 'What's yon queer thing?'

'A skeleton.' He wished she would go away.

'Bones, you mean. I saw one when they killed the big whale out at Byrehills. They sent the head and tail to the Castle to be salted for the Cardinal. The gulls ate the rest.'

'This is a human skeleton.' He added, to frighten her, 'Maybe a man who was hanged.'

'Tchah! You canna frighten me. I've seen one before, painted on the Cathedral wall. It had eyes and was grinning like a bogle. The priest said it was the Dance of Death.'

She flung the jerkin over his head. 'Come through with you now and get your breakfast. We've work to do.'

The first slow, limping walk that David took was to the end of the pier. He sat down there to rest his foot, dangling his legs over the barnacled wooden piles, and gazed towards the Castle.

Tiny figures moved on the ramparts and sunlight glinted off the bronze cannon. The bay was empty except for two fishing-boats and the gulls that wheeled and screamed above them.

In the quiet morning it was hard to believe that the Castle was held by murderers and outlaws. More than a month had passed since the Cardinal died, and the Regent and the churchmen were still squabbling over who should bear the cost of the siege.

David hobbled back to the quay. There was time for one more look at the medical book before he returned it to the canon.

It became more tedious every day to work at the nets. As his foot grew stronger, he began leaving his work to stroll along the quay and talk to the fishermen.

One morning in the first week of July he did not even bother to pick up the coils of twine and the meshing-pin. He lounged on the upturned bucket outside the hut, and Mahound squatted in his shadow. The monkey's excited squeaking made him open his eyes. Elspeth was looking at the unmended net.

'So you've not been working this forenoon.'

'No,' said David guiltily.

'It doesna matter. There'll be no more this week. I kent fine you'd weary of it once you could walk. It's dreich work for you.'

Her kindness embarrassed him still more. He said gruffly, 'I shan't be able to, tomorrow, anyway. I'm going up the town to buy a horse.'

'A *horse*!' she laughed. 'You'll not catch fish with a horse, David.'

'The horse is to take me to Leith.'

Elspeth dropped her fish-creel. 'Are you going away?'

David knelt and helped her collect the lines and pieces of bait that had dropped out of the basket. 'Not at once. Perhaps – perhaps next Wednesday.'

'It'll be queerlike without you,' she said, in a small voice.

'Well, I haven't gone yet,' he replied irritably. She looked at him in a forlorn way, and he stood with the lines awkwardly bundled in his hands. He had not expected Elspeth to be upset when he went away. He was even more glad that she had not found out they were cousins; strangely, at the same time, he could hardly stop himself from telling her.

As he hesitated, an extraordinary figure appeared on the quay. He was a pikeman, a huge, swaggering fellow. He called out to the fishermen as he approached them. By his speech he seemed a Scot, but he was dressed like a German mercenary in blue and purple slashed breeches, and he wore a Spanish steel helmet.

'It's one of them,' whispered Elspeth.

The fishermen fell silent as the pikeman came near.

'We want some fish at the Castle,' he said. 'What have you got?'

'None for the likes of you,' called someone at the back of the crowd. There were a few guffaws and the pikeman grasped his weapon.

'There's some in the boat down there. Fetch them.'

'Fetch them yourself! Or go and fish for some more.'

'Who said that?' roared the soldier. He lowered the point of his fifteen-foot pike and the fishermen fell back. The pikeman blustered and advanced menacingly; but he seemed afraid to begin a fight with so many.

As they all stood growling at each other like stiff-legged dogs, Mistress Binnie walked along the quay carrying a basket. Before Elspeth could run to her grandmother the pikeman had stopped her and pulled the lid off the basket.

'Eels,' he grinned. 'These'll do fine.'

'Lift off your hands, you thieving limmer!' shrieked the

old woman, and beat feebly at his face. The fishermen laughed as they tussled, and the pikeman laughed too.

'Och, you hell-cat!' he roared in mock rage.

'I'll fetch my dagger,' said David. Elspeth held him back. 'No, just hope she'll let him have them. Dinna anger him.'

The old woman screamed and spat, until the pikeman became angry, because he could not shake her off. He raised a fist to strike her.

'Go canny,' warned a fisherman. 'She'll wither your arm to the bone. She's a witch!'

David stared at the old woman in horror. So that was it – she was a witch! He stepped back.

The pikeman, too, leapt back as if he had been bitten. Mistress Binnie staggered against the wall, taking the basket with her. The eels poured in a writhing heap on the ground. They wriggled among the nets and lobster-pots, and one of them slid under the pikeman's feet. He missed his step and fell on top of his pike.

Mistress Binnie sat panting with rage. 'Dinna touch me!' she hissed, as Elspeth tried to take her into the hut.

The fishermen whooped and ran about the quay with sticks and rope-ends, trying to hit the swarming eels. Two of the younger men doubled their fists to punch the pikeman in his face and stomach.

'Over the side with him, lads!' they shouted. A dozen more left the eels and seized the pikeman. They heaved the struggling man in the air and threw him into the harbour. Someone brandished his pike and threw it after him.

The jeers and yells suddenly stopped, and the fishermen crowded to the side of the quay. They stared downwards, into the empty harbour. A low-pitched, unending groan came up from the mud.

The old woman had gone into a delirium of rage and curses. 'Can't you make her go inside?' said David. He could not bring himself to touch her.

Elspeth bent down and tried once more to coax her grandmother. Unexpectedly, she stood up, and walked without help into the hut. David followed nervously, still horrified at what he had learnt about her. Mistress Binnie collapsed at once on to her heather bed. Her head nodded and her eyes were glazed. She still cursed the pikeman under her breath.

'I'll fetch Father Anthony,' said David, glad of an excuse to get away. Outside, he looked to see if the canon was anywhere near the lepers' hospital. The fishermen were still clustered on the edge of the quay, listening to the horrible, uninterrupted moaning that came up from the mud.

David saw the canon by the Sea Port in the Priory wall. He limped towards him and told him what had happened. Father Anthony ran to the quayside and looked down into the harbour.

'This is more urgent,' he said to David. 'I'll see Mistress Binnie later.' He turned angrily to the eldest fisherman. 'James Cargill, are you all heathen Turks?'

'Father, he tried to master us, and –'

'I don't care what he did! Who will help me lift him out?'

The fishermen looked at each other and muttered. One of them spat at the twisted figure in the mud.

'I'll help you, Father,' said David.

The canon gave him a quick nod. 'First pass me my instruments.' He looped up his robe and clambered down the ladder on the harbour wall. David lay flat on the quay and dropped the case into Father Anthony's hands.

'Fetch me some fresh water. Some sticks as well – flat ones – and some rags.'

David went back to the hut. The old woman lay snoring, her eyes half-closed. David explained that the canon would come in later, and told Elspeth what he wanted. While he went to search the warehouse for some wood, Elspeth took the wooden bucket to the burn. As he turned the straw over, David thought, 'Why on earth am I doing this?'

He took out some thin lengths of wood and found the fishermen still at the edge of the quay, curious and sullen, but now very quiet. The pikeman had stopped groaning. He writhed from side to side, clenching his fists.

'Throw the boards down,' called up Father Anthony, and waded through the mud to pick them up. 'I need some rags to wipe away the slime. Can you help me?' He held out his hands to the fishermen, but none of them answered.

'I have some,' cried David, and to his astonishment, found himself hobbling back to the hut and using his dagger to tear apart his blue velvet doublet.

He climbed down the wall-ladder, grimacing every time his left foot touched a rung. A terrible smell rose from the greasy mud as it squelched under his bare toes.

Elspeth returned with the bucket full of water. David went back to the ladder to help her down, and the two of them stood by while the canon sponged away the foul-smelling slime from the man's face and clothes.

'I have to see if he is bleeding,' he explained.

The pikeman opened his eyes and began to curse Father Anthony with fluent obscenity. The canon took no notice.

'David, hold this fellow by the ears while I clean his face.'

One of the pikeman's arms was twisted under him. The other struck at David while he knelt by his head. The canon pinned the free arm with one hand and went on with his work.

Elspeth squatted in the mud. 'I'd like fine to stuff some of that dirt into his mouth,' she said fiercely.

'Instead you will please fetch me another bucketful of water from the burn. Make sure it comes from above the tide-mark.'

Elspeth obeyed meekly.

The canon began to feel the man's limbs and body. 'Good. Only the one arm and leg broken, as I thought at first. You were lucky not to land on a rock, man.'

The pikeman raised his head and spat in Father Anthony's face. 'There's some wax for your altar, you Pope's knight!' he cried hoarsely.

The canon wiped his cheek. 'I'll have to put your leg into splints. Have you a physician in the Castle? If not, you'd better listen to me, unless you want to lie in your bed for six months.'

He began to give some instructions. The pikeman listened with frightened eyes, although he went on cursing.

'Can you tie the rags into strips, David? Help me tie the splints.'

He explained and worked at the same time, binding the broken arm tightly against the chest, and strapping one leg against the other, with a splint along the broken limb. The huge body twisted under their hands and fought them like an unbroken horse.

'Lie still!' shouted the canon. 'You're giving yourself more pain.'

In the end the pikeman relaxed, his eyes closed.

'He's fainted,' said Elspeth in astonishment. The three of them looked down at the prostrate body.

'We'll need a board to lift him,' said David.

Elspeth said grudgingly, 'You can use our door if you bring it back.'

They left the canon beside the pikeman and dragged the heavy piece of wood over the quay. The fishermen stood back to let them by, but did not help them. They pushed the door over the edge; it smacked the mud with a sound like a pistol-shot.

'Gently,' said the canon as they tried to slide the door under the pikeman. They moved it an inch at a time, afraid of jarring the broken arm and leg. David began to sweat, and his arms shook with the strain of holding up the oak timbers. At last the man lay on the door as still as if he had been on his bier.

Father Anthony looked up at the quay. 'Who will help carry him to the Castle?'

Not one of the fishermen moved.

The canon shrugged and bent down again. With David and Elspeth he tried to lift the enormous load; but they slipped in the mud and almost tipped the unconscious man off the door. David gulped; he hated himself for not being as strong as the men who watched in hostile silence.

'Let's try again,' said the canon.

It was no use. They fumbled round the edge of the door, knowing that they could never lift it. There was a whisper and movement above them.

'All right, Father,' growled the fisherman named James Cargill. 'We'll give you a hand.'

He and two others jumped down without using the ladder. The canon waved David back. He stood aside unwillingly, although he knew the canon had done it because of his foot. The four men each took a corner of the door and between them lifted it easily. They began to wade through the mud to the ramp by the pier.

David frowned. He still could not understand why he had worked so hard to help the pikeman. He called after Father Anthony, 'I hope he thanks you before you leave him at the Castle!'

The canon looked back over his shoulder. 'He won't,' he said calmly. 'He'll start cursing me if he comes to his senses by then.'

CHAPTER SEVEN

A Meeting on the Sands

FOR several days Elspeth was afraid to leave her grandmother alone in the hut in case more of the Castilians came down to the harbour.

The old woman herself would not go outside. She sat by the cooking-pot, and fed the fire with peat and dried seaweed until the air was thick with smoke and Elspeth and David had to run to the door, with streaming eyes.

David was longing to go up to the town to look for a horse, but he made himself bear the long, tedious hours until Elspeth felt it was safe to leave the old woman on her own.

'I can come fishing with you now,' he said.

She shook her head. 'Not in the boat. We'll see what we can catch off the end of the pier. I'll not go out in the bay till I'm sure she's safe.'

She also refused to go up to Master Reid's house. Their meals during this time were meagre, and for the first time David went to bed hungry.

During the second week in July the weather became thundery. The sky still pulsated with heat, but its colour had changed to a dull, luminous yellow, and there were mutters of thunder out to sea. Every movement was an effort; nothing thrived but the flies on the middens.

Father Anthony came to see Mistress Binnie twice a day. 'I think she's suffered no harm,' he said.

Elspeth looked him straight in the eyes. 'Not in her body.'

The canon nodded, but said nothing. David could see that the old woman's wits were wavering even more than a month ago. For a few moments she would talk sensibly about the fishermen's families, or Mahound's latest prank; then she would bob and mutter for hours on end, safe in her own world.

On the fourth day after the eel incident David could bear it no longer.

'I must go up the town. I want to buy a horse.'

'Go then,' said Elspeth. 'There's no danger now.'

'We'll go fishing tomorrow,' he called back.

At the top of Kirk Hill he overtook Father Anthony. He had never planned how to buy the horse and now he wondered if the canon would be able to help him.

'Do you know anyone who might sell me a horse?'

'Come with me as I visit my patients. Someone may know of one for sale. Don't be too hopeful. The Castilians have stolen most of the saddle-horses in the town.'

They walked on together until the canon stopped outside the Castle gates. 'Here is my first patient. I must ask for news at the postern.'

David was aghast. 'That ruffian!'

'He's still my patient. I must make sure they are looking after him properly.'

As they crossed the footbridge over the ditch David's eyes went to the eastern blockhouse. On the newly-mortared stones was a dull brown stain. He shuddered as he reluctantly followed the canon to the postern.

The men-at-arms on the ramparts looked down at them indifferently and no one came to the gate. After moments of calling and knocking the wooden shutter opened. David's heart contracted; he wondered if Martin had come to the postern.

The voice was unfamiliar and uttered some rough insults. The canon glanced at his black robes.

'As you please, my friend. But how is the man who broke his leg?'

There were more voices inside the door, a hurried mutter, a laugh, and the first voice changed its tone.

'Bide there,' it said ingratiatingly. 'I'll find out.'

They were left alone for several minutes. The flies buzzed over a dead dog in the Castle ditch; there was a faint clank of metal inside the courtyard.

Suddenly they heard footsteps and shouts on the ramparts above them. David looked up and seized the canon's arm.

'Come back!' he shouted, and dragged Father Anthony to the bridge as a shower of stinking filth spattered round them. Some of it fell on their backs and shoulders.

'There's your medicine, you shaven devil!' The jeers of the men-at-arms pursued them across the bridge.

Father Anthony's face was white and his eyes burned. But he said nothing.

'The foul swine!' raged David. 'May they roast in torment for ever!'

They reached the safety of Castle Wynd and the canon put his hand on David's arm.

'No, David,' he said. 'No. I could be angry, too. It does no good. Control yourself. We can wash at the first house we visit.'

David groaned with disgust at his soiled jerkin. 'How can it happen in a Christian country? In France the king would have sent his fleet and army within a fortnight. Why do the Scots take so long to start the siege? Is the Regent a heretic, too, Father?'

'The Regent was jealous of the Cardinal's power. He

was jealous because the Cardinal took more thought for the things of Caesar than the things of God, and had more power than himself. He is slow, perhaps on purpose. But he is not a heretic.'

David was shocked. Laymen could say what they liked, but it was different for a priest. He had never heard a priest criticize his bishop before.

'It was a sin!'

The canon followed his disjointed thoughts. 'A deadly sin – as murder always is. I fear there will be more murder to come if we do not change our hearts. Every day I pray God to direct some Prince of the Church to purge us. *That* was no way to do it. Killing the Cardinal won't bring back that poor arrogant soul, George Wishart. It won't mend our parish churches, or stop our half-starved country priests from robbing their people –' He stopped abruptly. 'I've said too much. It's easy for me. My work is plain, whatever happens.'

He stooped under the doorway of a thatched house that faced the Mercat Cross. 'I've a dislocated shoulder to attend to in here. Come in and let me see if you have learnt any anatomy.'

They visited a dozen of the canon's patients, and at one house they were offered bread and cheese for dinner. Some of the houses were broken-down hovels, and some belonged to well-to-do craftsmen or merchants. Their visits all began in the same way. There was silence when they knocked; then a furtive opening of shutters and suspicious looks. At last, the canon would be recognized and the whole household come to greet him.

Father Anthony treated them all alike, only altering his tone to reprove the women when he found the middens piled high by the doorway.

'It's good muck, Father,' said one housewife indignantly. 'What we dinna put on the garden we can sell to the bailies. If we move our midden other folk will steal it.'

'They never learn,' said the canon wearily. 'Then they wonder why the rats come and why the plague strikes in summer.'

In the first house they were given water to clean the filth from their clothes, but at every visit the canon asked for more, and washed his hands.

'Why do you do that?' asked David curiously. 'There's no dirt on your hands.'

'None to see. But some may be clinging to my skin. It is dirt, David, that causes most of our ills.'

'Monsieur Perigord, our physician in Bordeaux, says that illness is carried by contagion in the air. He seals the rooms his patients lie in.'

'Indeed? In my experience, it's best to fling the windows wide, unless the weather is intolerably cold.'

The conversation took place in the house of James Brown, the Deacon of the Bakers, who had running sores on his leg. The canon had given David a bottle of salve and fresh bandages to hold as he inspected the leg. The Deacon swivelled his eyes nervously from one to the other.

'Is this lad your apprentice, Father?'

The canon smiled. 'No, Deacon. We doctors don't have apprentices. We study for many years and then we practise.'

The sick man turned to David. 'I saw you with the St Leonard's lads, last year. Are you to be a physician, then?'

Startled, David stared at the linen in his hand. He thought of Monsieur Perigord in his magnificent velvet and furs, who had half a dozen apothecaries and barber-surgeons to shield him from his patients and bring him their symptoms for analysis. He laughed.

'I, a physician?'

The canon watched him intently, as if he were straining after some hidden thought in David's mind. David felt the thought turn over, far down, like a fish glinting under a boat. He could not lay hold of it, but it frightened him. He made a joke to hide his confusion.

As they were leaving the sick baker rose on his elbow and called out, 'Come inby, Richard!'

A dark-browed young man entered and stared at David and the canon in an unfriendly way.

'Aye?' he grunted.

'Where's my wife, Richard?'

'How should I ken?' He walked out.

The Deacon apologized. 'Yon's my new prentice. I had him from Henry Reid and he hasna right settled since. He's a wee thing sullen.'

David was surprised that the apprentice dared to be so insolent. The Deacon called out again, 'Madge, are you there?' and his wife entered.

They whispered together and she went out to fetch a small canvas bag.

'Here, Father. It's not much, but it helps when the food's so short. It's only oatmeal.'

The woman handed the bag to the canon. 'Father, if only all the Cardinal's priests were like you! My sister's priest in Cupar took their cow for the death-mass when her man died, and cursed her at the altar when she couldna pay her tithes.'

The canon stood with bowed head.

Her husband put out a hand. 'Wheesht, Madge!' he cried, scandalized.

The canon said, 'Good-bye. Thank you for the oatmeal.' Outside, he handed the bag to David. 'They feed us well at the Priory. Give this to Elspeth.'

There seemed to be no horses for sale in St Andrews. Some, who had had a horse, took them to the stable to prove that the animal had gone. Others said they would not sell for a thousand French crowns. The town might become too unruly to live in and they would need a horse.

David became depressed at the constant refusals. He stopped to rub his foot which was beginning to ache. 'I'll walk to Crail. I could hire a boat there.'

'You've not yet asked Henry Reid,' said the canon. 'He bought a bay gelding before he sailed to France. I hear he's bankrupt since he lost his merchandise. Perhaps he'd be glad to sell the horse.'

David scowled. He could not forget that Master Reid had lied about him and advised the Binnies to get rid of him after the Cardinal's murder.

'I'd never ask *him* for a favour!'

The canon mopped his pale face, smeared with dust and sweat. He looked very tired. 'He's a good-natured man, David, though timid. He'd be pleased to help you now.'

David scowled even more, but said nothing. They walked back to the harbour and Father Anthony went in through the Sea Port of the Priory.

Mistress Binnie was alone in the hut. David looked at her warily; but she seemed to be in a sensible mood. He sat on the opposite side of the hearth, and she said, 'Elspeth is at the end of the pier.'

David gave her the bag of oatmeal and started playing with Mahound while the old woman wetted the meal to turn it into bannocks. As he teased Mahound with the gold tassels from his purse he wondered if the old woman would accept some money.

'I want to settle my debt.'

'Oh, aye?' The old woman looked up brightly.

He undid the purse strapped round his waist and pulled out a handful of silver, not counting it. 'Take this.' He pushed it at her quickly, afraid that Elspeth would come in.

Mistress Binnie did not seem to understand. 'Would it not be safer with yourself, laddie?'

'It's for you – a present!' said David impatiently. With dismay he saw that her eyes had dulled and her head was bobbing from side to side. He had another idea, and he began to burrow under the heather of the old woman's bed. He thrust the purse as far down as he could. When he went away he would take a few coins for his journey and leave the rest. Elspeth would not find it until she changed the heather. By that time he would be far away, his conscience appeased and his debt settled. He was very pleased with his scheme.

'I've hidden it there. Don't tell anyone.'

Mistress Binnie nodded eagerly. 'Nobody'll finger it there. I'll wither their arm if they touch it, like yon roistering soldier that took my eels.' Her yellow fingers clawed at David's arm. 'Did you see the bonny darlings leap out when I told them to trip him? I'll see to anyone that touches your siller, dear laddie.'

Her eyes sparkled with malice and David, horrified, backed away. Elspeth might have laughed at him, and Father Anthony, too. Most of the time he could tell himself that Mistress Binnie was only a muddled old woman whose mind glowed and faded like a dying peat fire. But his terrors now were not to be quenched by that kind of argument. He scrambled out of the hut and ran down to the sea.

He ran along the Priory wall, past the Shore Mill, across the bridge that spanned the Kinness Burn as it flowed into the harbour and over the waste land to the East Sands. He forgot all about the ache in his foot until he arrived panting at the rocks by the Kinkell cliffs. He tore up handfuls of wet, salty sand, and threw them across the beach, until he was more ashamed than terrified, and he wondered what the old woman thought of his sudden flight.

Above the cries of the sea-birds he heard a faint, hallooing shout. A man with a bundle was stumbling across the sands towards him. With his free hand he waved and went on shouting, 'You, you there, laddie!'

David stared, not believing his eyes. It was Martin.

Martin did not recognize him until he was a few yards away. He stopped disconcerted.

'David!' The low, shocked whisper seemed to last for minutes. Then he ran forward and seized David's hands, babbling and laughing. 'I didna ken you. You look so different. I thought you were dead. He only said a fisher-laddie brought the velvet –'

'Talk sense, man!' shouted David, trying to hide his joy. 'What velvet? What fisher-laddie?'

Martin undid his bundle. Inside were the rags of the blue velvet doublet that had been tied round the pikeman's splints. 'When they brought him in I kent it was your doublet. There's two of the gilt buttons still on it. He said –'

'Who?'

'Jock Carstairs, the pikeman. When he'd done cursing, he said they came from a fisher-laddie by the harbour. I couldna come before. Today Norman sent me out on a message.' His eyes darkened. 'I thought maybe you'd been killed on the rocks and someone had found the doublet in the sea.'

David held out his hand. 'Martin, I'm sorry we quarrelled.'

Martin grasped the hand. 'Let's not cast out again. Tell me what happened.'

They sat down on the sand and David explained about his foot and his unsuccessful search for a horse.

'We've plenty of beasts in the Castle stables, but it would cost my life to get you one.'

The delight faded from his sallow face; David saw that it was lined with misery. In a low voice, digging his fingers into the sand, he began to talk about his life in the Castle.

They had been brisk and jubilant to begin with. Norman had organized them to man the guns and oil the arquebuses and cross-bows in the armoury, to exercise the horses, to work in the bakehouse and kitchen.

When a summons had arrived to order them to appear before Parliament, Norman had laughed and torn up the safe-conduct. He said they would hand over the Regent's son in return for a free pardon. The kirkmen announced that only the Pope could give them pardon.

'I've been listed with the others as an outlaw. Didna you hear Lyon Herald proclaim it at the Mercat Cross?' He shivered.

'Then you regret the Cardinal's death?'

'No! I still think they were right. There are many godly men with us, David. There's James Melville and the Regent's own chaplain. They read the gospel to us and preach in the chapel. Yet the others –'

'Drink and dice, and let off their cross-bows at the

seagulls? What have they done with the Cardinal's body?'

Martin choked on his words. 'In – into the Castle midden. Then, because it was hot, they packed him in salt and wrapped the body in lead. It lies somewhere in the Castle, I think.'

He clutched his friend's arm. 'You're right, David, I *am* a coward. I canna swear and swagger. If only the Regent had come at once! I could have fought then. But I canna bear this waiting. They laugh at me and call me their pot-boy. They make me draw their wine ... And my mother will have no one to bring in her oats!'

He put his head between his hands and broke into harsh sobs. When he could control them he lifted his face defiantly. 'You laugh to see me greeting like a lassie.'

'No, Martin. It's not your fault you haven't any stomach for it. Why don't you leave them?'

'Where would I go? Nowhere in Scotland. We are all outlaws.'

'Come with me to France.'

Martin's eyes brightened, but grew dull again. 'I canna. They'd be after me. I ken when they're to send their letters to the English court.'

'They'd never catch you if we rode together. Take two horses from the Castle stables. We'll ride to Leith and find a ship for France. My father will give you work in Bordeaux.' He remembered what Martin had said to this offer before.

'I'd like that fine,' said Martin uncertainly. 'But I dinna see how I'll persuade the grooms to let me take the beasts out.'

David tried to encourage him. 'Where's your glib tongue, man? You can make up some excuse. I'll go to the Tolbooth every day at noon until I hear from you.'

Martin nodded and they walked up the beach to the grass hillocks that fringed the upper harbour, among the fishermen's nets spread out to dry. Martin kicked at the clumps of marram and thyme.

'You're a good friend, David. I said some stiff things to you in the Castle.'

'We were both angry. When we reach Bordeaux, you must guard your tongue. My father doesn't like Lutherans.'

'Aye, will I – until I get to Geneva.'

'Let's get to Bordeaux first!'

In an awkward gesture Martin put his arm round David's shoulders. 'It's all so clear in books, David. Out here it becomes mixter-matter. You canna seem to choose the good without the bad. I wish we were back in St Leonard's.'

David looked at him sadly. 'It seems so long ago. Do you remember how we had to bring our clubs here when the St Salvator's men were playing on the west links? The College Regents were afraid we'd fight.'

'I shall never swing a club again,' said Martin gloomily. 'The worst is, it doesna seem to matter.'

'I wonder what happened to Aristotle.'

Martin's head jerked in amazement. 'Aristotle?'

'The College laundress's dog. Don't you remember? She lent him to us to find the balls. He'd go and sit beside them when we'd played a stroke.'

A grin spread over Martin's face. 'Aye, I mind now. I havena taken him out since you left the College. He answered to "Aristotle" when we played at the golf, but as soon as we got him back on the street, he'd only come to "Blackie".'

'You used to say that it was only Aristotle's logic!'

Martin threw back his head to laugh at the bad joke. 'Aye, did I! Great days, David!'

They had reached the foot of Kirk Hill. 'Remember, now,' said David, 'tomorrow at noon, at the Tolbooth.'

Martin's face clouded. 'I'll do my best. But maybe not tomorrow.'

'Then the next day, or the next. Good-bye, Martin.'

Anxiously David watched his friend walk away. His bent shoulders shook as if he were laughing again at his joke. Then they drooped and his steps lagged up the steep hill.

'Holy Mother,' prayed David, 'let him be brave enough to do it.'

CHAPTER EIGHT

The Bargain

THE sky was lowering and plump with rain, but the storm had not yet broken. David threw the bucket of slops into the harbour and sat outside the hut. He ground his heels into the dust.

For seven days he had gone to the Tolbooth at noon and Martin had not been there. No message had come to the hut.

Almost worse than the suspense was his misunderstanding with Elspeth. On the first morning she had asked him to come out with her in the boat. He refused, afraid of missing Martin, and she had not asked him again. Her annoyance increased each day; but she did not ask him for an explanation. Obstinately David told himself that he would not be the first to mend their quarrel.

She came out of the hut. He had noticed she had gone to the boat later every day, as if giving him the chance to change his mind, although she always pretended not to notice him sitting by the door.

Suddenly he stood up. There was no point in going to the Tolbooth again. 'Elspeth!' he called.

She quickened her steps and the fishermen on the quay grinned. David ran after her. 'Wait! I'm coming with you.'

She swung round, her hands planted on her hips. 'He'll come today, his lordship says. What makes you think I want you?' The tone was deliberately coarse, but her face showed her unhappiness.

'Let me come, Elspeth,' he pleaded. 'I've been waiting for someone in the town. That's over now.' He nerved himself for what would follow. She would refuse at first. When he had begged and apologized enough she would let herself be persuaded. No girl could resist the chance.

Elspeth looked hard to see if he was telling the truth, and then, with no signs of resentment, asked him to go back for the wooden bucket. Mahound was squatting inside it. David swung it to and fro, and when the monkey refused to jump out he carried him along to Elspeth. She laughed as she saw her pet in the bucket. Walking beside her, David wondered if Marie of Bordeaux would have forgiven him so easily.

'Aren't you taking the boat?' he asked.

'No, the sky's too thick, and I wouldna like to be caught out there in a thunder-shower. Let's go along the braes and look for mussels. The best ones are out by the Eden, but I dinna care to go so far today.'

They crossed the waste land in front of St Nicholas's Leper Hospital and took the path up to the Kinkell Braes. They were soon high above the city; below them the sea oozed among the stumps of curving rocks, where the waves had eaten away the older cliffs. Elspeth pointed to a small beach between two reefs that jutted into the sea.

'We'll begin down there.'

They scrambled down a landslip, clinging to turf and gorse roots. Mahound jumped out of the bucket and Elspeth took it from David.

'We'll hae to fill this with water. That way we'll keep the mussels fresh. You can throw in any wee crabs you find as well.'

They worked across the tide-line, searching the drift-wood and bladderwrack and small rock pools. Then they prodded the shingle under the two ledges of rock, working out from the beach until the water came to their knees.

'There're not many here,' said Elspeth. 'Let's go on a bit.'

They moved from cove to cove until they reached a solitary pillar of rock that had stood unbroken when the tide drove back the line of cliffs. They had collected half a bucketful of crabs and mussels.

David finished his ledge first. He sprang up and sat on top with Mahound beside him. He watched Elspeth, and for the hundredth time he wondered what she would say if he told her that they were cousins.

At last she straightened herself and carried the bucket to the shore. She splashed back through the water to him.

'Help me up, then,' she laughed, and stretched up her hand. She leapt nimbly as he pulled her and sat down beside him. 'None of your fine Bordeaux lassies could jump like that,' she said.

David's heart gave a sudden jolt. 'They'd get a whipping if they tried to!'

'And it's one of those you'll be marrying?' she teased.

David stood up and ran to the end of the reef. He stared into the deep water and wondered why Elspeth could make him feel so foolish. She mistook his action.

'David, dinna jump in! The currents are chancy just here.'

He had never intended to, but her anxious voice made him reckless. He stripped off his canvas jerkin and tightened the knotted rope round his waist. He dived in with a flourish and heard Elspeth give a scream.

'I'm all right,' he shouted boastfully as he threshed the water. 'I'm a good swimmer.'

The current sucked at his legs and the rocks were sharp under the seaweed. He decided to swim to the next cove, and struck out from the reef, while Elspeth scrambled over the rocks on the shore, calling out advice and warning. Her nervous admiration made him swim far farther than he had meant to; he began to feel exhausted, and as he turned back to the shore, he saw Elspeth shrink against the cliff-face and cover her eyes.

'What's the matter?'

She shuddered and pointed across the rocks. He could see nothing unusual, but above the suck and chuckle of the sea he heard a dull, sustained buzzing. He waded up the shingly beach towards Elspeth, who was shaking with fear.

'There's a body over there!'

David looked over the tumbled boulders. Where the noise came from he saw a long, humped shape, and a black swarm of insects teeming above it. With nausea he remembered what Martin had said about the Cardinal's body. 'It lies somewhere in the Castle, I think.' *I think.*

He made himself step forward, but Elspeth clutched his arm. 'It's the currents. They set in here from the bay. David, dinna go to look.'

'I must.'

He crunched over the pebbles. For a moment he stared down at the heap of eyeless carrion, pecked by the gulls. The bones already gaped through the flesh. He gulped at the stench. Then he came back to Elspeth and put an arm round her.

'It's only a dead seal.'

She looked ashamed. 'I'm sorry, I thought it was a man.' He had to bend down to hear what she said next. 'I didna think of it when I watched you swim. But I minded as I came past the rock. They found my father's body just here.'

David kept his arm round Elspeth as they walked back to the beach where they had left the mussels. The first drops of rain began to splash on the sea, and even Mahound seemed to shuffle behind them in a subdued way as they returned to the harbour.

They had passed St Nicholas's and were nearly at the bridge when they saw a crowd by the harbour wall, and a curl of smoke twisting up from the Binnies's hut. They ran across the bridge, ignoring Mahound's cries, and raced along the Priory wall to the quay.

The crowd was not so large when they arrived; most of the noise and movement came from its centre, where a dozen soldiers had nearly finished pulling the Binnies's hut to pieces. The rubble walls were half demolished, and on the earth floor inside the rafters poked through the smouldering thatch like the ribs of the dead seal.

Elspeth screamed and flung herself at the soldiers, her fists pounding on their leather doublets.

The fisherman called James Cargill grabbed David's arm as he tried to follow Elspeth. 'Dinna be a fool, laddie. They'll ding your head off. They came for more fish and the old wife ran out to curse them. They've broken the lassie's skiff already.'

David shook him off and ran forward. One of the soldiers hit him on the cheek; at a shouted order the whole group formed up and marched towards Kirk Hill. Two of them carried a wicker basket full of fish, slung on their pikes.

The fishermen crowded round the ruined hut where the rain hissed as it dropped on the smouldering reeds and heather. Mistress Binnie was huddled in a corner and the overturned cooking-pot had made a puddle by her feet. The burning peats had been kicked round the floor.

Elspeth put her arms round her grandmother. 'Could none of you have stopped them?' she shouted. The fishermen stood like a row of gulls on the quayside, as if they were afraid to show any sympathy. Elspeth looked desperately from one to the other.

'She canna stay here in the rain. Can one of you take her in?'

The men muttered to each other and began to move away.

'It might be our turn next,' said one. In a few moments they had all gone.

'David, what can I do?'

'There's always the warehouse,' he said, looking helplessly round the wreckage.

'We canna all three bide in there!' She began to sob so violently that she jerked the old woman from side to side. 'I shouldna have left her, I shouldna have left her!' she kept crying.

David crouched beside them, unable to bear Elspeth's grief. 'Elspeth, stop it! I'll go away and the two of you can live in the warehouse.'

She clung to his arm. 'Please dinna leave us. They might come back. Go up to Master Reid. He'll take us all in. Go quickly, David. She'll catch a fever if she bides out in the rain.'

David's face hardened. 'But ...' Then he rose to his feet, and began to run up the steps of Kirk Hill, trying to reach the merchant's house before his grievance made him turn back.

He ran up the forestair and thumped the oaken door.

'Master Reid!' he yelled, brushing the rain out of his eyes. 'Master Reid, open your door!' He tried to turn his anger into urgency for Elspeth's sake and hammered on the wood without a pause. 'Come quickly! I have a message from Elspeth Binnie.'

At last the door opened a few inches on an iron chain. The merchant peered out cautiously. 'David Lindsay?' he said doubtfully. He unhooked the chain, pulled David in, and barred the door again. His face was thinner and his sandy beard straggled more than ever. His eyes moved disbelievingly over David as he told his story.

'I hardly kent you! ... Poor souls, poor souls. Homeless, in weather like this. They must come here at once. Bring them –' He stopped and fingered his beard nervously. 'Why did you say the Castilians pulled down their hut?'

Angrily David repeated what the fisherman had said.

'Aye, well,' muttered Master Reid. 'They might think to come here, too. Then where would *I* be? I'd like to help them. But it's not as if I was a strapping young callant like yourself.' His face became shrewd. 'Maybe there's a way. Here, I'll strike a bargain. I'll take in the womenfolk – and their thieving ape as well – if you'll bide with us.'

David looked at him in incredulous contempt. He had bitten back his pride to help Elspeth, but nothing would make him stay in the merchant's house himself. He would rather sleep on the quay.

'I can't come. I'm leaving St Andrews soon.'

The merchant's voice became calculating. 'I'll not put myself in danger for anyone, Master David. You're a braw strong birkie. You can help protect my house if there's need. That's my bargain. You bide here or I'll not take in the Binnies.'

Sick-hearted, David tried to convince himself that Master Reid was bluffing. 'For how long?'

'So long as the Binnies are here, or until the Regent routs those murdering loons out of the Castle.'

For a moment they stood weighing each other's intentions. David wondered what Father Anthony would have done, and he wished as he had never wished before that he could push the choice away. He heard the rain drumming on the forestair, and remembered the look on Elspeth's face as she appealed to the fisherman.

He said at last, 'All right. I shall stay.' He turned to the door and fumbled for the chain. Master Reid's hand fell on his shoulder.

'A man must think of himself,' he pleaded. 'They'll sleep better here than they ever did in yon hovel. Davy!'

David flinched at the familiar use of his name.

'What?' he said roughly.

'Davy, I've kept your lute safe for you. It's in the best chamber, wrapped in a piece of silk. You'll be blithe to have it back.'

When he returned to the harbour Elspeth and the old woman were still sitting inside the wrecked hut. They seemed not to have moved, although the rain had drenched their kirtles, and Elspeth's hair hung in glistening, heavy locks.

David bent over her. 'Is there anything we can take from here?'

She lifted blank eyes. 'From *here*?'

David turned over the piles of heather and opened the wooden chest. He found nothing. Either the soldiers had looted thoroughly or the Binnies had owned nothing except their clothes and cooking-pots. The feel of the heather under his hands reminded him that he had hidden his purse in the old woman's bed. He swore and began to rummage frantically, not caring whether Elspeth saw him or not. He found only a silver penny that was lying under a broken pitcher.

'What's the use?' cried Elspeth shrilly. 'Let's go.'

David shrugged. It was too late to curse his stupid action now. He retrieved his dagger from the warehouse and helped Elspeth pull Mistress Binnie to her feet, while

Mahound, who had now come home, whimpered and scratched among the dead ashes.

It was little more than a quarter-mile from the harbour to Master Reid's house, yet it seemed the longest journey he had ever made. The old woman hung slackly on his arm; when she moved of her own accord, it was only to struggle down the hill.

'Come on now, come on,' Elspeth tried to coax her. 'You'll soon be out of the rain.'

Her eyes were bright and her lips moved in silent words. Her mind seemed to have run away from the unbearable present, but her body was with them and fought all their efforts to take her to safety.

'David, I canna go on,' gasped Elspeth. 'She's too heavy for me.'

'Siller,' suddenly cried Mistress Binnie. 'The laddie's siller. I must fetch it.' Once more she tried to go back to the harbour.

David put his lips to her ear. 'The money's safe. We've got it with us. Come along, now.'

The old woman gave him an affectionate smile and began to walk almost briskly between them. Elspeth was too tired to ask for an explanation.

CHAPTER NINE

The Regent Arrives

FROM the first, David found it hard to resist the merchant's kindness and the comfort of their new life. After the smoky, low-roofed hut, there were three rooms where one could walk without stooping. The furniture was solid Dantzig oak, and they ate off pewter.

'It'll be safer to put the womenfolk between us,' said Master Reid. He placed Elspeth and the old woman in the middle room, his own bedchamber. He himself slept on a mattress in the small apprentice's room at the gable-end and gave David a truckle bed in the hall, where they cooked, ate their meals, and sat in the evening.

During their first meal David sat in obstinate silence. Master Reid refused to notice his sullenness; he laughed, called him Davy, and kept trying to draw him into their conversation. By the end of the evening David had relaxed. He smiled and talked to Master Reid, and when they went to bed he fell asleep, full of guilty relief, with his hands smoothing the linen sheets.

Next day, Master Reid pointed fussily at his guests' ragged clothes. 'I can dress you all better than that. Elspeth, get you into your chamber and take a kirtle from my wife's old chest by the window. Find a kirtle for your grannie as well.'

For David he brought out shirt and shoes, with a doublet of light brown and green hose. The doublet had a deep-cut neck and laced breast-piece that had been out of fashion for twenty years. Knots of scarlet ribbon hung from the shoulders.

'I was as slim as yourself when I wore this.' He plucked off the ribbons with an awkward smile. 'You'll not be wanting these. I wore them at my wedding, when we danced behind Holy Trinity.'

Oddly touched, David took the clothes down to the bakehouse. As he stripped off the fisherman's jerkin he hoped that Elspeth would not be offended. He walked up the forestair clumsily; the unaccustomed shoes weighted his feet like cannon-balls.

On the threshold of the hall he stopped in astonishment. Elspeth stood by the fireplace, sleek-haired, dressed in a dark red kirtle. Her fingers pulled anxiously at the sleeves. She looked pleased, but anxious.

'It's queer,' she said to Master Reid. She glanced quickly at David and away again. He remained dumb with amazement at the change in her.

The merchant said, 'Poor Katharine would be glad for you to have this as well, my doo.' He put a silver chain round Elspeth's neck. Her face glowed.

'Well?' she challenged David, with a smile. He stood tongue-tied. Her face changed.

'Did you think I *liked* having only one ragged kirtle?' she cried angrily. She ran into her bedchamber, banging the door. Master Reid laughed at David's bewildered face.

An hour later Elspeth came back to the hall and began to cook their meal. From working in the house, she knew the place of every pan and dish, and she moved round it as if she had always been its mistress. Master Reid remarked many times how much she resembled his poor Katharine, who had died ten years ago. David stared and stared. Several days passed before he could speak to Elspeth in a natural voice.

Master Reid's stock of food was low. Now, as they all knew, it would disappear four times as quickly. As the skiff had been wrecked by the Castilians, Elspeth was not able to fish in the bay. Master Reid said that he would ask the Deacon of the Bakers to let him fire his oven again. But the Deacon refused. He said the other bakers would protest. Since Master Reid had set himself up as a merchant he must take the consequences.

'It's yon Richard Strang behind it all,' said Master Reid. 'An insinuating devil, he is! I ken James Brown would never refuse me if he wasna being pushed.'

He went round each of the bakers in turn, asking them to let him share their work in the communal bakehouses. When they said 'No', he offered to work for a wage as a journeyman. They all refused him.

Each evening Elspeth and David looked tensely at each other as Master Reid opened the door. His face told them at once that he had failed again. They began to dread his dejected return and the gloomy meal that followed it.

Mistress Binnie, once installed in the bed in the middle room, refused to leave it. David heard her squabbling with Elspeth in the morning when she tried to wash her grandmother's face and hands before she ate.

'She'll not rise at all,' cried Elspeth in despair. 'Soon she'll not be able to.'

One morning, David left the house secretly to look for some work. He soon found that the craft rules would not let him be taken on by any skilled workman, and that the casual tasks found in any port or great cathedral city had ceased entirely since the Cardinal's murder.

When he returned home Elspeth was facing Master Reid as if they were in the middle of an argument. 'Dinna be daft,' she scolded him. 'It has to be. We have to eat.'

Master Reid spread his hands helplessly. 'Och, very well, then. But you'll have to do it yourself. I canna.'

Elspeth tied an apron above her red kirtle and went

down the garden. Master Reid leaned out of the window.

'Not the sitting ones!' he cried after her. He said to David, 'My wife stocked the doocot. This was her father's bakehouse – I was his prentice. She aye had a notion to a doocot, and I promised that when we inherited –'

There was a screeching from the bottom of the garden and a white flock of doves billowed into the air. Elspeth returned breathless. Two limp bodies filled her hands.

'I'll do better next time,' she said. She put a hand on Master Reid's arm. 'I'm gey sorry,' she said gently. 'They were bonny creatures.' The merchant looked at her like a small boy being consoled by his mother. David suddenly felt that he should not have been in the room.

They had been living in the merchant's house for a fortnight when the fisherman, James Cargill, knocked at the door. 'I want the laddie,' he said to Elspeth. His red face opened in amazement when he saw David's changed appearance.

'Have you still got your old duds?' he asked. 'You can come out in the boat with me, if you like. You'd take your share of the catch.'

There was no time for thanks and he did not seem to expect any. David ran down to the bakehouse where he had stuffed the fisherman's clothes behind the kneading-trough. James Cargill looked him up and down dourly.

'You'll have to work,' he said, and nothing else until they reached the harbour.

From that day David went with James Cargill whenever he took his boat out to sea. Sometimes he went by day, sometimes by night, depending on the tide, and whether he had stake-nets to set for salmon in the Eden, or was fishing for cod in the bay. David suspected that the fishing-trips varied for another reason. Next to hauling in a good catch, Cargill liked best celebrating it in a city tavern.

David did not dare to protest. At whatever hour his knock and bellowed, 'David! David! Do you hear me?' came to the door, he would stumble out of bed, pull on his canvas breeches and go out in the darkness.

He was a bad sailor; but he fought his nausea, his lack of sleep, and his agonizingly blistered hands, for the sake of the few fish that he could take home for Elspeth.

He was given other food when he went round the town with Father Anthony. Not very much, and less and less as the weeks went by, but it was still enough to keep them from starving. He grinned wryly to himself sometimes as he thought of the strange turn his life had taken: an old woman, a girl, and a middle-aged merchant all depended on him for food, when three months before they would have been as strange and indifferent to him as the one-legged men in Africa. However, he did not think about this much. He was too busy.

One day as he walked with Cargill and some other fishermen to the harbour they saw in the bay two ships gaudy with pennants and banners. The mizzens flew the white St Andrew's cross on blue, and from the mainmasts fluttered the red lion rampant. The leading ship carried the royal arms of Scotland.

The two vessels sailed steadily towards the harbour; they rode low in the water and their decks were piled with wooden barrels, pikes, and glinting pieces of armour.

James Cargill shouted like a man gone mad. 'Run for the Provost, lads! Run to the Tolbooth and ring the bell. They've come at last – the Regent and the Queen are here!'

But the Regent had not yet come. Only the Queen Dowager and her household had arrived in the two ships, with a few men-at-arms to escort her. They lodged at the New Inns of the Priory, and the streets in daytime were full of silks and velvet, as if the court had come for a late summer visit.

While the Castilians shrank back into their fortress, the citizens waited for the detachment of Lothians men who were to serve the first twenty days of the siege. At the end of three weeks the Lothians men marched home and the Regent had still not come. Rumours went round St Andrews: the Queen had spoken angrily to the bishops and noblemen about the Regent's cowardice. If he did not appear soon, she cried, she would begin the assault herself.

At last, in the middle of September, the Regent, Lord Arran, arrived with his wife and another army from Forfar and Kincardine. Two huge cannon, Crookmow and Deaf Meg, were dragged overland from Crail by oxen. It took thirty-six animals and nine drivers to pull each gun. The slow, creaking carts, moving two miles in every hour, took the baggage and ammunition to the fields west of the Castle, where the army lay encamped near the edge of the cliffs.

David went with Father Anthony to watch the beginning of the siege. They saw two cannon and some smaller guns drawn up about three hundred yards from the Castle wall. Behind the gabions, the wickerwork screens packed with earth, the crews were stacking their baskets of cartridges and gun-stones in the trenches. The slow-matches were already burning on the linstocks, and they had rammed in the first charge. But the soldiers looked uninterested. They sat outside their tents to dice, or mend equipment. The whole field had been churned into a mire by the baggage-wagons.

The canon did not seem impressed by what he saw. He

pointed to a group of arquebus-men who were casting their bullets round a charcoal brazier. 'They had to strip the roof of Holyrood for that lead. How King Francis would laugh at them! Does the Regent think he has come to knock down a wooden barn?'

David stared at the great stone ramparts of the Castle and thought about Martin.

'Can they hold out against artillery?'

'Of course not, if the Regent used his guns properly. They are fifty-pounders. He should aim them into the inner courtyard. But trained like this!' He pointed scornfully at the cannon. 'The west wall is strengthened with earthworks.'

'Why doesn't the Regent attack the front of the Castle?'

'Because you must protect your gunners with trenches and gabions. How could he dig trenches in Castle Wynd? Besides, the houses would block his line of fire.'

He strode away impatiently and David followed. So he missed the opening shots. He heard three explosions in the distance, followed by cheering and a clatter of falling stones. Later he heard that the first salvo had taken some slates off the Castle roof.

David wondered where Martin had been when the guns were fired, but without much emotion. His anxiety had become dull over the past weeks. Sometimes he forgot to pray for him.

It became clear that it would take more than a few cannon-balls to breach the western wall, and a company of crossbowmen was sent to the cliffs east of the Castle. Their bolts shattered the large windows of the hall and chapel, and the sound of breaking glass was heard all over the town. But the Castilians soon nailed boards across the gap. After two days they began to return the fire. They turned one of their own guns against the camp. The six-inch gun-stone killed an ox then bounced towards the tent where the Regent was planning the campaign. After that, a protective line of wagons encircled the tent and the gabions were built even higher.

The courtiers and the army had brought their own food, but the citizens still went hungry. The harvest was not yet in; although the countryfolk were coming into the town again, they had little to sell. It would be a long time before the meal-chests and the barrels for salted meat were full again.

One afternoon David returned from the harbour to find the apprentice, Richard Strang, sprawled across Master Reid's forestair. Strang was twirling a stick in his fingers. He poked the string of fish that David carried over his arm.

'Best keep to your fishing, laddie. Leave baking to them that kens the craft.'

David pushed him aside and the apprentice hooked an arm round his legs. 'Get out of my way!' said David. 'Why are you on our stair?' He raised his hand to lift the latch and Strang ducked back, shielding his face.

Inside the house was Strang's new master, the Deacon, James Brown, and a tall bearded man in black velvet, who was smiling indulgently at the two smaller men as they bristled fiercely at each other.

'You canna do it,' roared the Deacon. 'It's against the burgh laws, Harry. I dinna care if the Queen herself commands it.'

Master Reid glared back. The man in black held up his hand and waved his embroidered glove. 'My friends, your city regulations are tiresome. Monsieur Deacon, I have been kind to you long enough. Go!' Smiling, he pushed James Brown towards the door.

The Deacon went away, grumbling bitterly, 'It's a different cry when the court needs our taxes.'

'*Bon*,' said the man in black. 'Now to our affairs, Monsieur Reid.' The merchant pulled forward a stool, but the visitor waved it away. 'No, thank you. I have to be with her Grace at three. Listen. The wheat will come from the Priory mill already ground. We do you this favour because the Priory bakehouse cannot supply all our needs. You will bake as if the bread were for the Queen herself. You understand, yes? There will be no mixing of oatmeal or other flour.'

Master Reid said stiffly, 'Sir, we St Andrews bakers are forbidden to make oaten bread. We bake only wheat and rye.'

'You will deliver the bread daily to the New Inns . . . Is this lad your apprentice?' He looked disapprovingly at the string of fish and David's ragged clothes.

David flushed and Master Reid threw him an imploring glance.

'I can bring the bread, if you wish, monsieur.'

He had answered in French; after a brief flick of surprise, the man said, 'Good. Monsieur Reid, you may keep each tenth loaf for your payment, to sell or eat yourselves. Now, *mon Dieu*, what else was there?'

David gritted his teeth. Master Reid waited respectfully.

'Ah, that girl! A neat, tidy creature. She is – how do you say – good with her needle? Yes?'

Master Reid and David exchanged glances. The merchant said hastily, 'Aye, sir. What's your pleasure with her?'

'Lady Arran needs another sewing-maid. Send the girl along to the house in Southgate, where the Regent lodges, tomorrow.'

Master Reid ran to open the door. After the man had left the smell of musk remained in the room. The merchant sat on the stool his visitor had refused. He beat his knees gleefully.

'Davy, that was the Master of the Queen's Household! Someone told him I was the best baker in St Andrews. I'm to bake for the court. My luck's turned at last!'

David felt a surge of impatient affection. 'What happens after the siege?' he wanted to ask. 'What happens when there's no one to help you against the burgh magistrates?'

He was not going to spoil the merchant's pleasure. So he asked instead, 'What about Elspeth? She's never used a needle in her life.'

'I didna want to displease him.' Master Reid looked troubled. 'She'll ken how to sew. Every lassie does.'

'Does she know how to hem cambric shifts and bed-linen?'

'Aye,' said the merchant unhappily, 'maybe I've been a wee thing rash.'

David was alone in the hall when Elspeth returned from her errand and he told her what had been arranged for her. Her eyes darkened. Then she set her mouth firmly and said with a little too much confidence, 'I ken fine how to sew. My mother taught me.'

She bridled at David's incredulous look. 'My mother wasna a fisher-lassie,' she flashed. 'She was a Lindsay of Pitcairnie.'

CHAPTER TEN

The Mine

WHEN the flour came from the Priory mill two soldiers walked beside the cart and stood on guard while the driver unloaded his sacks at Master Reid's bakehouse. David saw a crowd of apprentices and young bakers following the cart down Castle Wynd. They were led by Richard Strang, who stood as near as he dared and tried to rouse the others against Master Reid.

There were some angry mutters, but not the riot he seemed to have hoped for. The crowd dispersed and Master Reid was ready to begin his baking.

'We'll hae to bolt the flour, then get some firing for the oven. I'll go and cut some whins on the common. Elspeth, afore you go to Lady Arran, cry on the maltsters in Northgate and see if they'll let me have some yeast.'

'What can I do?' asked David.

'Stick to your fishing, Davie. Last night the old wife said she'd come down the stair to help me. It will keep her from fretting at the guns, and there's not work for four.'

David put on his fishing clothes and went down to the harbour feeling slightly displeased that he had not been asked to help in the bakehouse.

He heard later that none of the maltmen would sell any yeast to Master Reid. He begged some from the Priory bakehouse, but when it arrived it was sour. Master Reid sat groaning beside his kneading-trough. Elspeth reported their difficulties to Lady Arran's housekeeper, who spoke to the Master of the Queen's Household. Within an hour six brewers' men had called at the bakehouse and they were promised more yeast than they could use.

At supper Master Reid told this story a dozen times. Elspeth smiled at his compliments, while her grandmother nodded away like a bobbing apple. 'She's a clever lassie,' she kept on saying. Once she added, with a sly look, 'There's no burgess wife could guide your house better, Henry Reid.'

The merchant glowed down to the roots of his sandy beard. David scowled and left the table abruptly, pleased to see Elspeth's look of concern. A moment later he came back to his stool, muttering in excuse, 'I wanted to give some fish to Mahound,' and he whistled and snapped his fingers at the monkey, who was chewing a salted herring by the fire. Elspeth watched David closely for a moment; then she smiled to herself and spoke to her grandmother.

Two days later he returned from a night trip with James Cargill. There was frost in the morning now; he was chilled to the bone and thinking longingly of the bakehouse fire and the new, steaming bread. In the raw, grey light, he saw Elspeth struggling down Castle Wynd with two buckets of water. They were so heavy that however carefully she walked the water splashed on the road and over her kirtle. David took them from her. Elspeth rubbed her shoulders and joked, 'I'm the bakehouse water-boy.'

David felt wildly angry with Master Reid. 'Why can't he fetch the water himself?'

'It's the prentices. Yesterday they jostled him off the common when he went to cut whins for the oven. Now they'll not let him get to the wells.' She coloured. 'They dinna hinder me. I ken how to manage Richard Strang. He was aye about me when he baked with Master Reid.'

David's hands clenched round the bucket handles. He

would have liked to tear Richard Strang to bits, as Mahound had torn the salted herring. 'I won't go out fishing any more. I'll help in the bakehouse ... Why didn't you tell me? You know I want to do anything I can for you.'

'Do you?' Her eyes were kind, but there was a strangely regretful look in them. She kept her thoughts to herself. 'Here, you can help by setting the water on the fire for me. Dinna let it boil. Just blood-hot it has to be.'

They began to cross the cobbled space in front of the bakehouse. Where the plastered wall rose from its stone footing, letters had been daubed between the black beams along the whole side of the house. Elspeth exclaimed and touched the wall. Her hand came away smudged with charcoal.

'Master Reid went to complain to the Deacon about the prentices a wee while before I left the house. It canna be long done. What does it say, David?'

He was glad she could not read. He ran to look up the street, but saw nobody. 'Let's get some rags and rub it off before he comes back.'

'What does it say?' persisted Elspeth, as they scrubbed the plaster. David obliterated the most obscene words before he answered. The rest was a spiteful, senseless insult.

'It says, "THEY ARE ALL LUTHERANS IN HERE".'

They had been baking for only a few days when they saw a troop of soldiers leading some ponies into the garden of the house next to Master Reid's. It stood on the corner of Castle Wynd, and belonged to a cooper and his wife, who had three small children.

'The cooper and his family are leaving,' reported Elspeth. They saw the man and his wife pulling a small handcart piled with bedding and cooking-pots up the street.

'I've taken a list,' screamed the woman at the soldiers. 'I'll have the Privy Council at you if you skaith my kitchen-gear!'

The soldiers unloaded their own equipment: picks, shovels, planks of timber, and bales of fodder for the ponies. They stowed all this in the various rooms of the house. One of the men grinned at David as he stood looking over the wall.

'Will you lend us a hand, laddie? We're going to dig a mine.'

'Where to?'

The man jerked his thumb. 'To the foretower of the Castle. So they say. I dinna ken if it can be done. It's solid rock down there.'

They began by excavating a pit in the topsoil; then they drove a wide tunnel into the rock. Soon most of the engineers had disappeared underground, and the ponies plodded in and out all day with lanterns strapped to their panniers, bringing up the broken stones.

After the first excitement David and Elspeth lost interest. It was slow work; only the mounting pile of debris showed that the mine was creeping steadily nearer the Castle, and there was little activity on the surface.

But one morning the Castle guns, instead of firing at the Regent's battery to the west, roared overhead. The Castilians had guessed what was happening and had turned their cannon against the engineers.

The cooper's house soon lay in ruins. The soldiers were unconcerned. It was not their house and the extra rubble helped to protect the entrance to the mine. The bakehouse tables rattled every time a cannon-ball thudded into the cooper's garden. Mistress Binnie would run out and shake her fist.

'The pest on you,' she screamed at the Castle. 'I'll bring the pest on you!'

At first the Regent's soldiers were amused. They leant over the garden wall and jeered while David and Elspeth pulled the old woman back to safety, away from flying splinters and stones. But once a culverin shot took the head off an Aberdeen man as he stood laughing by the wall. His body fell into the cooper's garden and his head rolled across Master Reid's bed of parsley. David hurried Elspeth indoors. He heard one of the men shout, 'Curse you, you old witch! The devil helped you with that!'

The soldier jumped over the wall, picked up the head, and ran back to the mine. None of them came near the wall afterwards.

As the mine debris rose higher the Castilians pounded continually with their guns at the entrance. They killed some of the ponies and three of the soldiers, but the work went on. Towards the end of October the tunnel had reached the Castle ditch. The engineers reported the sound of picks tapping on the other side of the ditch, as if the Castilians were making a counter-mine. So the soldiers prepared a minehead at the end of the gallery, from where they could run two or three smaller tunnels towards the foundations of the Castle. If the wall did not collapse at once, they would blow it up with gunpowder.

Their work had to stop for a few days when they struck a seam of coal. The chief engineer was afraid that water seeping here might bring down the tunnel roof; so the Regent sent for coal-miners from south Fife to cut back the face correctly and prevent a fall. At the same time the chief engineer and a French officer in the Queen's Household disagreed about the direction of the tunnels they were to run from the minehead, and the Regent could not decide which plan to follow.

The soldiers loitered at the mine entrance and diced, while they waited for their masters to agree, and an unlucky cannon-shot from the Castle wounded six of them at once.

It was impossible to move the men before their wounds were dressed. Wooden screens were put up to shelter them from the guns, and someone sent for Father Anthony. David heard the groans of the wounded men and went out to help.

He saw the canon bending over a man whose right hand had been torn off by the gun-stone, and ran to join him. He had not spoken to Father Anthony for a fortnight, for the canon had seen how busy David was and had not taken him to visit his patients in the town.

Father Anthony smiled, but only said, 'Hand me my forceps, David.'

They worked together almost in silence, searching and dressing the wounds as quickly as possible. The mess of blood and torn flesh at first turned David's stomach; then he managed to control his shaking hands; he handed over the instruments, and salves, and bandages, or held down the twitching limbs as the canon instructed him.

At last their work was finished. Some men-at-arms removed the wounded soldiers on hurdles to the camp, and one stayed behind to rake earth over the blood-soaked remains of the accident. Another cannon-ball whistled over their heads.

David asked hurriedly, 'Father, will you come into the house?'

'No, thank you, I have to go to someone in Southgate now. But I have something for you. I was bringing it here when I was asked to come to the mine.' He handed David a letter.

'You remember, in June, I arranged to send a letter for you to Bordeaux. Here is your answer.'

David recognized his father's handwriting, but stared at it stupidly. 'How could it come here?'

'The master of the *Giroflée* brought it to the Priory. I wrote to your parents myself to say that your wound wasn't dangerous. Your chest of books and clothes has come in the ship as well. I told the sailors to deliver them to Master Reid's house.'

The *Giroflée* in harbour! David's heart pounded.

'Is she here for long? When does she go back to France?'

'Tomorrow, when she has unloaded her wine.'

David considered the news. His excitement died away and he shook his head. 'I think I must stay here. Master Reid needs me in the bakehouse. I'll wait till the siege is finished.'

Perhaps by Christmas, he told himself. There would be many other French ships in St Andrews harbour by then. 'I shall write to my father and tell him I am staying here.'

'Shall I take the letter to the ship for you?'

David flushed. He remembered the insolent, ill-mannered boy who had tormented the crew of the *Giroflée*. It would be awkward meeting them again. He hoped the master had forgotten his impertinence.

'No, thank you. I must speak to the master myself. My father will want to know that he has seen me.'

His father's letter made him homesick, but it did not change his plans. His father advised him to stay in St Andrews for a time and make his interest with the new Archbishop. He hoped that David's wound was now cured and that he had found comfortable lodgings in the town.

He mentioned several noblemen who would be pleased to help a cousin of Lindsay of Pitcairnie.

'He hasn't heard that Lindsay of Pitcairnie is with the Castilians,' thought David.

At the end of the letter, David read, 'We hope you will reward the poor fisherfolk who have tended you in your illness. The master of the *Giroflée* holds certain moneys on which you may draw to pay their expenses. Give them our thanks.'

David stuffed the letter inside his shirt as hastily as if the words had been spoken aloud. Now he would never be able to put matters right with Elspeth. He should have told her at once that they were cousins. If he told her now, she would despise him for keeping silent: she would guess his reasons only too clearly.

But he could tell his parents. His father was rich and still had many connections in Scotland. He had a strong sense of family duty. If Elspeth had been on her own he would probably have asked her to live with them in Bordeaux. But that was unthinkable: the Binnies must never know the truth. He hoped his father would understand his embarrassment. He could do something for the Binnies; perhaps buy them a house in St Andrews.

David's conscience was not quite satisfied, but he told himself it was the best he could do. After all, he would soon be leaving St Andrews. It would do Elspeth no good to know they were cousins, since she would never see him again.

He wondered for a moment why the thought made him so depressed. Then he went into the bakehouse and began to knead the next troughful of dough.

The easterly winds blew sharply off St Andrews Bay in mid-November. In the morning the rubble at the mine-entrance was rimed with frost, and the ponies steamed like brewers' vats as they plodded in and out.

One day as the four of them huddled round the bake-house oven they heard an uproar in the cooper's garden. David ran to the wall. A fat, heavily furred man was sitting his horse among a crowd of angry soldiers. He listened to them with a frown and then rode away. The soldiers began to shout at each other.

'What's the matter?' called David.

One of the men spat after the rider. He yelled back, 'The Castilians have broken through, that's what. A counter-mine! They reached our minehead before we got to the walls. We've been idle all week because his bonnie lordship there, Jamie Arran, couldna make up his mind which road to dig! All yon work wasted!'

'Will you fill it in again?'

The soldier held up his red, blistered hands, and explained exactly how and with what the Regent could fill his mine. When he had finished he flung his shovel into a pile of earth and said bitterly, 'I'll lay you ten crowns they make us guard the break-through now. Thank the saints my time here is up at the end of the month.'

CHAPTER ELEVEN

The Truce

By the end of November it was obvious that the siege was going to last much longer than anyone had expected. Six English ships appeared in the bay. The Regent's guns stopped them landing supplies for the Castle, but messages passed by night in small boats.

'Did you hear that?' asked Master Reid, when at last the English fleet sailed away. 'They've taken Norman Leslie and some others with them. They'll be away to the English court. That means we'll have the English over the Border next year, and not a word that the French mean to help us.'

One cold, sunny morning, when David lifted the tray of bread he was to take to the New Inns, Elspeth came up to him, clutching Mahound in her arms.

'I'm to come with you,' she said, and her face warned David not to ask why. As they walked to the Priory gatehouse he wondered if she was ill. They were all eating more now, but he knew the old woman kept Elspeth awake at night, and the gunfire terrified her.

When they reached the guest-house, David said, 'I have to take the bread to the kitchens.'

'I'll bide for you by the front door.'

David delivered his tray to the pantryman. When he came back Elspeth was standing with her hand touching the bell-rope.

'I canna do it, David. You ring.'

Without asking why, he pulled the rope. Inside the hall

a crowd of servants and minor officials waited, each as near the fire as his rank allowed him. Someone of surprising importance came up to them and held out his hands. Elspeth squeezed Mahound so hard that he whimpered.

'Lady Arran said I was to see the Master of the Household.'

The man smiled at her fierceness and told them to follow him. David saw that Elspeth's eyes were full of tears. He hardly noticed that they had walked into a room full of courtiers and the Queen Dowager's ladies-in-waiting.

'Take off your bonnet, prentice,' commanded an insolent voice, and one of the young men tipped off his cap with a silver-headed cane. David glared at the smooth, tittering faces; he snatched up his cap, brushed off the rush-ends, and set it on his head again.

'Who lets such sweaty jerkins into the court?' mocked another voice. David's eyes blurred with anger. He stepped with clenched fists towards the lounging figure by the hearth. He heard Elspeth's frightened whisper, and at the same time smelt the odour of musk behind him. The courtiers' taunts died into silence: the Master of the Queen's Household had come into the room.

He smiled and cautiously scratched Mahound's red crest. 'A charming little creature. Her Grace will be pleased.' He frowned at Elspeth's distressed face. 'It is an honour for you, *ma fille*. I will give you something to sweeten the parting. Follow me.' He handed Mahound to another official.

Elspeth groped for David's arm and stumbled beside him down a corridor. They were led to a door opening on a small orchard. The Master of the Household pointed across the grass between the bare trees to a wicket-gate in a high wall. It surrounded another, smaller building.

'Go and wait by that gate. You may stay there until the clock strikes, and then you must go home by that pathway over there. Take this.' He pressed a leather purse into Elspeth's hands and shut the door behind them.

Elspeth's steps dragged across the grass. 'I took Mahound with me to Lady Arran's. She was gey pleased with him. She said she'd take him for her birthday gift to the Queen.'

'She can't! He's yours.'

Elspeth sobbed as she pressed her cheek against the stone wall. 'What way could I say no? It would make trouble for us all.'

They looked through the wicket-gate into an enclosed garden. The flower-beds were empty, but there were some late roses clustered among the rosemary against the walls, and a blackbird was sunning herself and whistling in the pale warmth of the garden.

'Let's go,' cried David, dragging Elspeth's arm. 'Does he think he's the Grand Turk, to order us about like this?'

They heard a burst of children's laughter. Through the door of the house ran five small girls, all about four years old, all miniature court ladies in brocade kirtles looped with gold and pearls. They tottered stiffly in their heavy clothes and kept looking back at the door, as if they had run disobediently outside.

'Marie! Marie! Viens ici, mignonne!' called a woman's voice. The five small girls shrieked with laughter and clapped their hands to their mouths.

'Marie! Marie!' they chanted, as they chased each other round the garden. *'Madame, nous nous appelons toutes Marie!'*

One of them faced her companions with an upraised

hand. The four-year-olds giggled and dipped in overbalanced curtsies. They fell into line behind their leader, who paced solemnly to the tall woman smiling in the doorway. Behind her was the Master of the Household. Mahound clung to his shoulder, now wearing a scarlet jacket and a silver chain on a belt round his waist.

They heard the small girl's scream of delight, and saw Mahound wriggle in terror as she pulled him down by the chain. Elspeth's fingers gripped the wicket-gate and she watched Mary Stewart pull her new toy round the garden.

'It's not right!' cried Elspeth passionately. 'Master Reid bought Mahound for me at the Senzie fair in forty-four. *She* could have a shipload of monkeys if she wanted.' Her face became distorted with jealous grief.

David put his arm round her. 'I'll send you another monkey, Elspeth. Two, if you like.'

The tears splashed down Elspeth's face. 'I dinna want another monkey. I want Mahound.'

They walked home as silently as they had come. David practised a dozen comforting sentences in his head, but none seemed right. Elspeth went to her room and stayed there until dinner-time. Old Mistress Binnie was surprisingly calm when she heard what had happened. She patted Elspeth's shoulder.

'There, there, my doo, you'll soon have other ploys to think on,' and she threw a sly look at Master Reid.

David spent the afternoon full of miserable anger, sieving three sackfuls of flour for the kneading-trough. He riddled as much flour on to the floor as into the storage barrel, and at last, Master Reid, who was annoyed at his clumsiness, told him to fetch some more whins from the common instead.

Mistress Binnie followed him outside. She had a message for the blacksmith's wife in Southgate, she said. David listened patiently. He hoped the blacksmith's wife could make better sense of the long tale than he could.

The old woman broke off with a scream. 'Look – it's him! The loon with the pike!'

There were three men half-running, half-staggering along the road from the Castle. One of them fell beside a midden and began to vomit, while the two others collapsed near the bakehouse. The nearest was the pikeman who had tried to steal Mistress Binnie's basket of eels.

His face was blotched and sweating, and he jerked on the ground as if in intense pain. They went up to him, but could see no wound. He clutched Mistress Binnie's kirtle.

'Give me some water, old wife. They turned us out of the Castle. Give me some water!'

The old woman went into the bakehouse and filled a wooden bowl with water. While she took it out to the pikeman David told Master Reid about the extraordinary scene outside.

The merchant wiped his floury hands, went pale, and exclaimed, 'The daft old fool!' He ran outside. 'Come inby at once, you gyte old besom!'

The old woman was kneeling by the pikeman, trying to pour the water into his mouth so quickly that David could not tell whether she meant it as a kindness, or was trying to choke him.

Six soldiers on guard at the mine-entrance came out of the cooper's garden and began to prod the other two figures with their spear-butts.

'Get away, you fools!' yelled Master Reid down the street. As David stepped towards Mistress Binnie, he grasped his arm in a frenzy of alarm. 'You're not to go,

Davy. If yon stupid carline doesna leave him this minute I'll not have her in my house again ... Janet Binnie, come here!'

The old woman took no notice. One of the soldiers suddently pushed his companions away, and at arms' length, ripped open the leather jerkin of the man sprawled across the midden. He inspected the man's armpits and his face changed. 'Hold back,' he said hoarsely. 'He's deader than the Cardinal. He's got boils on him.'

Before he finished there was a long muffled cry in the rubble behind them. A roar of terror reached them. 'Wat, Robbie, Dan! Where are you, lads?'

A man came leaping over the earth and stones, almost mad with fright. As David and Master Reid ran to join the soldiers, he said that he had been in the mine-chamber, posted there to raise the alarm if there was any movement in the counter-mine. He heard movements in the tunnel. When they stopped, he held up his lantern to the break-through and saw some long, shapeless objects on the floor of the counter-mine. He put his hand in and tugged at what turned out to be a knotted end of a sheet. He felt a hard lump inside the cloth. It was too heavy to pull down into the mine-chamber.

'It began to move.' The soldier shuddered. 'I'll swear someone pushed it. It landed at my feet, and another bundle with it. I couldna right see by the lantern, so I slit the sheet with my whinger, and it was – it was like yon.' He pointed to the dead man on the midden. 'The tunnel's full of them.'

'I telt you,' cried Master Reid shrilly. 'I telt you to leave him alone.' The soldiers drew away from the midden.

Mistress Binnie waddled slowly over the road with her empty basin. 'He's dead,' she quavered. 'A big strong man like him. Dead as a fish.'

The soldiers backed away from her. 'You touched him,' growled one.

Master Reid was sweating with panic. 'What about this one? I saw you open his jerkin. He's dead too.'

They formed into two hostile groups, with Master Reid confronting the soldiers.

'We've all been near them,' said David. 'We could all be infected.'

'There's not been time,' insisted Master Reid. 'Take it easy, lads. Let's all away home, and get the bailies to clean the street.'

The soldiers nodded in relief. 'Right,' said one. 'But mind, if there's trouble, the old wife was with him the longest. It's her blame.'

They separated. Mistress Binnie kept repeating tremulously, as they walked back to the bakehouse, 'I dinna understand. I didna touch him. He just gied a loup from the ground and died.'

Master Reid hustled her indoors. 'Of course he did,' he shouted. 'You daft limmer, do you not ken the pest when you see it?'

The news soon spread through the town. The three bodies were removed and buried in waste land outside the gates, and a fire was lit to clean the places where they had died.

Lady Arran departed for Kinneil House the same day, leaving her women to pack the luggage. Within a week, most of the court had fled from St Andrews. The Queen Dowager took her daughter to Linlithgow, the bishops and nobles melted away and, last of all, the Regent decided to lift the siege.

The entrance to the mine was boarded over; not very securely, because the soldiers said they could smell the pest inside the tunnel and would not stay to work there. They nailed a few timber baulks as quickly as they could, and hurried back to the camp, where the Regent had already given orders for the tents to be struck.

'He can't leave us!' cried David, when Father Anthony told him the news.

'It's true. He's made a truce with them. He's promised to let them keep the Castle – and his son – until they are absolved by the Pope.'

'How long will that be?'

'Nobody knows.'

They stood at the end of Castle Wynd and watched the seige-train depart. The oxen strained at the carriages of Crookmow and Deaf Meg, their hooves slipping on the frozen mud. The soldiers shoved cheerfully at the baggage-wagons: they had not expected to be home for Christmas.

The camp broke up, leaving only a waste of mud and midden-heaps. There was no movement on the Castle walls during the whole week that the soldiers spent evacuating the town, but every day Father Anthony came to stand in the street near the bakehouse, his eyes fixed on the Castle gates, as if he waited for some sign.

On Christmas Eve they saw the last piece of artillery being pulled towards the Crail road. As the cart creaked away, snow began to fall out of the grey sky. Father Anthony remained standing by the cooper's ruined walls.

'So they've gone,' said David bitterly. 'Did the Regent make them promise to leave the town in peace?'

'No.'

'Did they promise *nothing*?'

'Only one thing. That's why I'm waiting here. It can't be long now.'

David shivered. He stamped his feet for warmth and the snow-flakes settled on Father Anthony's black robes.

The postern-gate of the Castle opened and six men appeared, carrying what looked like a burst gun-barrel. Father Anthony stepped forward to meet them. The men trudged up the street singing and laughing as if they were half-drunk. David saw that their load was a roll of lead, roughly twisted over at the ends. It was as long as a man.

'They're taking him to Blackfriars Chapel,' said the canon. 'Will you come with me?'

David's mouth went dry as he stared at the lead.

'Not unless you want to,' added the canon. David was amazed at his calmness.

'I'll come with you, Father.' They fell into step behind the jostling, unsteady-footed Castilians. David walked with his eyes on the ground, trying to shut out the thick voices of the men in front. The canon's lips moved silently as he walked beside him; but David found he could not remember a single word from the Office for the Dead, not even the shortest prayer, for the funeral procession of Cardinal Archbishop David Beaton.

CHAPTER TWELVE

Martin

DAVID pulled the old frieze cloak round his shoulders as he trudged through the slush in Marketgate. The streets should have been full of children begging for nuts and apples, and neighbours wishing each other a good New Year. He had met only bands of apprentices with cudgels tucked into their belts. The city cleansers and searchers were out, too; at the corner of Foul Waste he met four of them with their white-tipped sticks. They were fumigating an infected house with brimstone and juniper twigs. A cauldron bubbled on the fire outside; one of the cleansers was using his stick to push a heap of clothes and bed-linen into the boiling water.

The bitter smoke made David cough, and he stepped to the other side of the road. The men shouted at him: one of their tasks was to keep people off the streets. Their voices were muffled by the vinegar-soaked cloths wound round their heads. David hurried by. Another wretched family had been sent to the pest-camp by the sea. The bailies would not let them settle by the Kinness Burn, in case they polluted the Priory mill-stream. So the huts had been put up for them near the archery practice-ground, on the links. David had heard the camp described by Father Anthony. There was a good water-supply from the Swilcan Burn, and the magistrates sent out food every day; but the low ground was swept by every icy blast off the sea.

David passed several houses in Marketgate with boards

nailed over the doorways. If the household survived their quarantine on the links without dying of the plague or the bitter weather, they would be allowed to return.

'If there's a house to return to,' David muttered to himself. Some of the empty houses had been looted by the Castilians, and one had been accidentally burnt down when set alight by a pan of charcoal left in the hall by the city cleansers.

He arrived at last at the house he was looking for and rapped on the door.

'What do you want, laddie?' asked James Brown, the Deacon of the Bakers.

'Yeast,' said David. He ignored Richard Strang, who lounged sulkily on a bench under the window.

James Brown looked nervously at his apprentice. 'So you've still got some of the Regent's flour, have you?'

'A little,' admitted David.

'Then you can bake yourselves unleavened bread!' roared the Deacon. 'Richard, go to Walter Edie and say I'll need him here at noon with his key to the Bakers' Chest.'

Strang scratched his thick black hair. 'You ken we're not supposed to be on the streets,' he whined.

'When has that hindered you?' shouted James Brown. 'Take as long as you like,' he added lamely, and David realized that the older man was afraid of his apprentice. With an unpleasant grin Strang left the room.

James Brown reached for a leather tankard. He held it out to David, and a strong smell of warm ale and spices rose up. 'Here, sup this. It's cinnamon, cloves, and saffron. It never fails to keep off the pest.'

'No, thank you. Can't you let us have some yeast?'

The Deacon went to look out of the window, made sure the door was shut, and then said, 'Harry Reid is my oldest friend. We were prentices together in that bakehouse of his, when it belonged to his dead wife's daddy. But he was born and reared in Cupar. He isna a St Andrews man.'

'What difference does that make?'

'See here.' The Deacon clasped David's arm and breathed the warm, spiced ale into his face. 'There's plenty of wild camsteery lads in the town spoiling for a fight. They'd take any excuse, now the magistrates canna hold the town in order. I'm telling you, Davy, you'd best hide that flour, or maybe one of yon nights your bakehouse will go up in a blaze.'

David looked at him indignantly. 'Can't you control a few apprentices? You, the Deacon!'

James Brown put out a shaky hand for the tankard. 'I'm busy seeing to the food for the poor souls on the links. It was Bailie Morrison's job, but he died of the pest two days syne. Then there's the Castilians roaring up and down the town. What with them and the pest, folk are feared to do anything but mind their own business. So, I'm warning you.'

'I see.' He turned to go.

'Bide a wee.' James Brown disappeared for a moment and came back with a twist of grey cloth which he slipped into David's hand. 'Take yon. But mind, there's to be no more.'

David thanked him and slipped the small parcel of yeast inside his doublet. In the doorway he turned round.

'Why does Richard Strang hate Henry Reid so much? And all of us in his house?'

A puzzled look came into the Deacon's eyes, as if David had questioned a simple fact of nature, like the way that yeast made his dough expand.

'Something inside him, I suppose. He's aye been thrawn. Dinna cross him. You'd better not meddle with him,

Davy. Get back to your studies and your friends at St Leonard's.'

'Not yet,' said David.

The street was very quiet, but he could hear shouts in the distance. It had been like that ever since the Regent left the town. The townsfolk quivered inside their houses, waiting for the next outrage: an ale-house looted, the thatch of an empty house set alight, some girl or elderly man tormented and insulted in the street. So far no one had been killed, but the incidents were getting worse every day. The Castilians were taking revenge for the four months they had been shut up inside their walls, and the young men of the town prowled behind them like jackals after lions.

The shouting came from near the Fish Cross in Northgate. David broke into a run, thinking of what the Deacon had said about the bakehouse. He found a yelling mob in the doorway of an ale-house opposite the Fish Cross. He was going to pass quickly, when he saw that half a dozen men were kicking someone on the ground, and that one of them was hitting him with a pot-hook and chain. He ran across the road and seized the swinging arm. The chain wrapped itself round his wrist, bruising it, and the attackers turned on him angrily.

'Gie him a clout, Wattie!' yelled the chain-swinger. The man lying in the slush scrambled to his feet and ran into Castle Wynd. David found himself struggling in the doorway. He cursed his interference; they were so crowded that the clenched fists could not reach him, but he was being pushed farther into the ale-house, and he was surrounded by the mob.

The dark taproom was full of shouting, jumping figures. On top of the table the town piper was standing and breathlessly squeaking out a Christmas carol. Someone prodded him with a dagger whenever he stopped. Crouched against the far wall were two girls, and one of them was Elspeth.

Later, David heard that the apprentices had come to drink at the ale-house, bringing the piper with them for some New Year music. The ale-house keeper's daughter sat on one of the apprentice's knees, and they were all enjoying themselves hugely. Then a dozen Castilians had come in.

The fight was fiercest round the two girls. The Castilians were trying to pull them out of their corner and the young townsmen had thrown themselves in front.

'Elspeth!' cried David, at the top of his voice. Shc heard him and tried to come to him. Richard Strang was in front of her, protecting her with no concern for his own safety, as David had to admit. Strang heard David's cry, glared across the room and pushed Elspeth back into the corner.

A choking rage, such as he had never felt in his life before, swept over David. He punched and kicked his way across the taproom, not caring whose face or body he hurt. When he reached Richard Strang, he shouted, 'Stand out of my way!'

The apprentice grinned and held Elspeth behind him with both hands. With a deliberateness that shocked him later, David tightened his fist and punched the young man twice, low in the belly. Strang gasped and sagged against the wall. With one arm round Elspeth, David fought his way back to the door, and the piper jumped off the table and followed him. Once outside, he found he was shaking with exhaustion and he could hardly support Elspeth's weight on his arm.

'I only went to get some ale,' she sobbed. 'Master Reid sent me to get a tankard of ale. Those men started daffing with Betsy and me. The baker-lads didna like it. One of them said they ought to let me alone, my grannie had broken Jock Carstairs' arm when he took her basket of eels.'

'What stupid nonsense!'

'One of the Castilians said she was a witch, she had put the ill on the town as well, and it was easy seen how the pest got round St Andrews, and he hoped it would rot the whole of Marketgate. Oh, David!' She cried for a few moments more, and then became calm. 'That's how the birlie started. You're not to tell my grandmother or Henry Reid. I'm all right now.' Almost shyly, she pressed his hand. 'David, thank you for helping me.'

David passed on the Deacon's warning to Master Reid. He looked worried and tugged at his sandy beard. 'Did you tell him we had those sacks of flour in the bake-house?'

'Of course not.'

'Good laddie. We'll have to hide them. I ken just the very place.'

At five o'clock, when the winter evening was dark enough to hide their movements, they carried the sacks up the forestair and hid them under the bed that Elspeth shared with her grandmother. David's conscience troubled him. The flour had not been paid for, and it belonged to the Regent.

'What use would it be to him?' demanded Master Reid. 'He's playing cards and cutting for King of the Bean in Linlithgow tonight. Na, na, let him come and fetch it. We'll not use that much, anyway. Just enough for our own bread.'

Later that night they heard shouting in the darkened streets. David rose from his truckle-bed and went to peer through the peephole in the door. He saw torchlight glinting off the muddy slush below, and at least twenty figures tramping up the street. He could not tell whether they were townsfolk or Castilians, but he heard someone whisper below the forestair and rattle the bakehouse door.

He suggested to Master Reid that they should sit up at night in turn, to make sure the roof was not fired while they slept.

'Aye, a good idea,' agreed Master Reid. They arranged to sit up for four hours each, timing themselves by the hour-glass that Master Reid sometimes used in the bakery. 'And you needna stir the womenfolk when you wake me,' said Master Reid. 'Just come down the forestair and up the ladder on the gable-end by my window. Give two whistles and I'll ken it's you.'

They did not tell Elspeth or Mistress Binnie about their arrangement, but Elspeth found out when David began to fall asleep over their midday meal. Now that they no longer baked for the court, he had rejoined James Cargill on some of his fishing expeditions, and he could hardly keep awake when he was sitting in the house.

Elspeth begged them to let her take her turn in guarding the house. She accepted David's refusal meekly, but she tried to wheedle Master Reid, clinging to his arm.

'Na, na, my doo,' he laughed. 'Ask me for ribbons or a stick of ginger, and I couldna refuse you. But not this.'

He patted her dark hair and a violent shock of anger made David's heart thump. He was startled by an urge to go up to Master Reid and pummel his face as he had done to the men in the ale-house.

Elspeth, quite unaware of what she had done, was now soberly clearing the table. David's eyes followed her about the room. He had a great deal to think of during his vigil that night.

January passed by. The Castilians looted and assaulted, and a few of the townsfolk were killed in the riots. The Castilians set fire to the houses in Prior's Wynd and gutted the church of the Blackfriars Monastery. A few letters, but no promise of help, came from the Regent.

If the night was clear and frosty, David could hear the noises in the Castle courtyard, only one hundred yards away: the clink of weapons, the shout of men on the walls, and the clatter of their feet on the bridge as they came out to look for sport in the town. Sometimes he heard singing in the Castle chapel. When he went round to waken Master Reid, he often saw lights in its windows. The chant of hymns made a strange contrast to the brawling sounds around it; but the singing voices were faint and almost drowned by the surge of waves against the Castle rock.

One night towards the end of February an uproar took place almost under Master Reid's windows. The man whose house had been raided had stirred up his neighbours, and the younger men had pursued the Castilians down Castle Wynd. A running fight was going on in the street. The shouts and sounds of blows went on for more than half an hour.

Master Reid came to knock on the front door and David let him in. The merchant went to a wooden chest and took out a blackened leather jerkin and a clumsy old sword with a cross-hilt. He fumbled with the straps and laces of the jerkin. David grimaced as he saw him sit down with the sword edge across his knees. He ran his finger along the notched edge of his duelling dagger. Neither of them would be much use against a dozen men-at-arms.

They sat by the cold ashes of the fire. David yawned and shivered stiffly. At last Master Reid said, 'There's still a great noise in the street, but it seems different.'

David listened. The babble of voices now sounded more like men arguing. 'I'll go and see what's happening.'

He slipped cautiously down the forestair and looked around. Two men with torches stood by the ruins of the cooper's house; a dark pack of men behind them was moving round the garden.

'Hey, you!' A weapon flickered in the torchlight and one of the men stepped towards him. 'Oh, you're not from the Castle, are you? You can help us. Walter Edie says he saw a man come out of the mine.'

'Jouked into it more like,' scoffed his companion. 'Why should anyone crawl through the pest-corpses when the gates are open?'

'The rest of them have jinked us into the Castle, so let's try for this one. I'd like to get my fingers round his thrapple. Off you go, laddie. Join the others in the garden. We'll bar his road this way.'

David stumbled over the uneven ground. Another torch flared on the other side of the rubble, lighting up the splintered branches of the apple-trees. The searchers moved slowly across the garden, thrusting their swords into bushes and patches of shadow. There was no chance that anyone hiding there would escape. The Castle guns had not breached the dyke at the foot of the garden, and a cordon of men was beating inwards from the wall.

David's throat began to contract with a cold, suffocating fear. He could think of only one reason why anyone should try to come out by the mine, escaping both townsfolk and Castilians. There was only one person who would want to do that.

As he walked with the line of beaters he strained his eyes for the slightest movement on the ground. But the torchlight blurred everything. It made darker shadows on the darkness and men were moving or swishing their sticks and swords all around him.

'If I were hunted like this,' he thought, 'I know what I'd do. I'd go back to the mine.'

He waited until a shout sent half the searchers stumbling to the other side of the ruins. 'Here, lads, I've seen him! Hunt the otter!' Then, praying that he had guessed correctly, he bent double and ran towards the mine.

The gap in the boards felt wider than he remembered. They came apart easily. There was a damp, sickly smell inside. He tripped over a shovel and fell full length on the rocky ground.

His hands were grazed, but there was no other damage. When he recovered his breath, David rose and groped forward. He heard a strange, panting sound.

'Martin?' he whispered, and the rock walls sent back an echo. He crawled forward in the darkness. His hand touched wet cloth, with the feel of a body underneath it. The panting had stopped. David groped over the front of a sodden doublet, and pulled open the fastenings. There was a flat, hard lump inside. His fingers recoiled for a moment, until he realized that it was a book. Underneath it the man's heart was beating.

'Martin?' he whispered again. The body, which had been as rigid as a paralysed rabbit, relaxed a little, and groaned.

'It's David, Martin.'

'Are they coming in for me?'

'No. We'll wait here till they've gone.'

They crouched in silence until the shouts and flickers of torchlight had disappeared. It seemed hours later to David when he tried to persuade Martin to leave the tunnel. Martin's teeth were chattering.

'I canna. They're watching for me.'

'Not now. They'll be away to their beds.' David thought hard. In Master Reid's garden was a range of wooden sheds: the pigsty, the cattle-byre, and a small stable. The animals had long ago been sold off to pay Master Reid's debts, but there was some straw in the byre and it would be warmer than the plague-reeking tunnel.

He looked outside. The frozen slush glimmered in the starlight and the dark shapes in the garden were now still. He gulped the pure, untainted air. 'Come on. There's no one here.'

He was relieved to find that Martin could walk without help. They stepped cautiously from the shadow of one broken tree to the next, until they came to Master Reid's wall. David sat on top and pulled Martin over.

'I canna leave town till the morning,' whispered Martin. 'I think I've taken a fever. They've flooded the countermine and I fell into the water.'

'I'll get you dry clothes.' David remembered that his clothes chest, returned by the *Giroflée,* stood in Master Reid's hall. He grinned sourly at the thought of dressing Martin in his own useless finery.

He led Martin to the stable and pulled the straw into a thick heap. 'Here, wrap yourself in that. I'll be back soon with the clothes and some food.'

Martin muttered his thanks. As he left him, David thought how odd it was that during the whole incident he had not once seen his friend's face.

CHAPTER THIRTEEN

The Castilians' Hymn

MASTER REID was still sitting by the hearth. He had stirred a glow out of the ashes, and put another turf on the fire. 'It was cold in here,' he explained guiltily. 'I hope Elspeth winna flyte at me for wasting fuel.' Lately, they had let the fire die out at night.

It was easy for David to tell only half the truth of what had happened outside. Master Reid went down the fore-stair to his own room at the far end of the house, and David waited for a few moments before he collected what Martin would need: dry clothes and shoes, a piece of bread, and a few salted fish. He also unhooked a lantern from its place above the plate-cupboard, and lit the stump of a tallow candle inside it. Once he thought he heard movements in the middle room and footsteps by the door. But no one came through. He put the bundle of food and clothes under his arm and closed the shutter of the lantern so that it would not give light until he reached the stable.

Martin grabbed the food, but David made him change his clothes before eating. By the lantern-light Martin's eyes were great black hollows; his hands that clutched the bread were as thin and wrinkled as Mahound's, and almost as dark with grime. When he began eating he seemed to find it hard to swallow.

'I couldna get the horses,' said Martin between mouthfuls. David's mind went back over the seven months since their last meeting. 'No,' he said shortly. He went to the bakehouse to fetch a pitcher of water. 'Have this. The fish will make you thirsty.'

Martin gulped down some of the water and began to speak very quickly, with his hands clasped round the pitcher.

'I thought after the siege I could just walk out. I didna care where I went. I'd rather be hanged than bide in there. But they wouldna let me. They call us "the chapel bairns". They say we'll all win or swing together. They even break in when we're at our prayers. There's just the dozen of us, David. The rest of them – I couldna speak of what they do! God has sent the plague to punish them.'

David offered him another piece of salted fish. Martin shook his head. 'It's queer. I hid for two days in the cellar below the guardroom, biding my chance to get into the counter-mine, and I hadna a bite to eat. Now I canna put the food down.'

'What are you going to do?'

Martin looked at him sideways. 'I'd like to go to France with you.'

David sighed. 'We wouldn't be allowed to sail from Leith if they knew we came from here – not as long as there's plague in the town. Besides, I can't go away just now.'

Martin pointed towards the house. 'Something in there, is there?'

'Yes. I can't leave them, Martin.'

Martin nodded despondently. 'I thought maybe it would be too late. I'll walk to Lindores. My mother will hide me till this steer blows by. Dinna fash yourself about me, David.'

He stood up and tried to go to the stable door, but immediately fell down with a surprised look on his face. 'I'm wambly in the legs. It must be yon two days without food.'

David said anxiously, 'You needn't go at once. Stay here for a few days. No one will come in here. I'll bring you some more food in the morning.'

Martin blinked his eyes wearily. 'Aye, I'll take a few hours' rest. But I'll not stay long.' He pulled out the book that had been lying inside his doublet, and held it to the lantern-light. The leather covers gleamed darkly with moisture and the pages were stuck together. All his misfortunes rose to his face as he tried to dry the edges near the candle-flame.

'Even my English Testament,' he said bitterly. 'Maybe I'll be drowned as I try to cross the Eden. That would make a fine end to all my misluck.'

David held out his hand. 'Give it to me. I'll dry it for you by the fire in the hall.'

Martin's face was full of suspicion. 'You'll let me have it back?'

'Of course, you fool! I'll stay awake until it's dry and hide it under my mattress. You'll have it back in the morning.'

Reluctantly, Martin handed over the small volume. 'Maybe it will be for your own good to read it. Maybe it was meant to be spoilt.'

'I don't intend to read it. Not because it's forbidden, but –' David sighed again, seeing the light of argument flare in Martin's eyes. 'Oh, what's the use? We'll never understand each other. I promise to keep it safe. Go to sleep.'

As he sat by the glowing peat carefully drying and prising open the damp pages, David began to realize what he had done. Martin might have to stay for several days in the stables before he was strong enough to walk to Lindores. He was a Castilian, and David had offered

Master Reid's protection both to him and his heretical book. He had no right to bring this extra danger on the household. Yet how could he have left Martin cowering at the mine-entrance?

He flung himself down on the truckle-bed, his eyes wide open, conscious of the hard lump of the English Testament under his mattress. He was still lying awake, trying to solve the problem, when the first grey light seeped through the wooden shutters.

He made an excuse to go down the garden soon after breakfast. He had only the heel of an old loaf, but Mistress Binnie was going to boil up soup from the few withered herbs left in the garden and he hoped he would be able to steal some of this for Martin. Before he reached the stable Elspeth caught up with him.

'He will not be able to move today,' she said quietly.

David's hand flew to the bread hidden inside his doublet. Elspeth pulled him towards the empty dove-cot. 'I saw you last night. I heard the noise and came to my door. Who is he?'

When David had explained, Elspeth said reproachfully, 'Did you not trust us?'

David flushed. 'It isn't that. It could be dangerous for all of you.'

Elspeth touched his arm. 'I keeked through the stable-door a few minutes ago. Your friend's sleeping. He doesna look well to me. He'd best come inby to the fire.'

'Master Reid wouldn't like it.'

'Let me see to it. He'll do it if I ask him.'

David's voice grated. 'Thank you, Elspeth.' She gave him a sad, penetrating look. 'Och, David, you are a daft laddie.' She laughed, but did not really sound amused.

When there was no one in the street they brought Martin up to the hall. He sat on a stool by the hearth, sharing the fire with the iron cooking-pot that was now always half-empty. Master Reid kept looking at him in a worried, exasperated way, but he pressed food on him which Martin said he did not want. He pulled a blanket round his shoulders and stared languidly into the red peats all afternoon.

When they were alone for a moment, David took the English Testament from its hiding-place and handed it to his friend. Martin thrust it inside the borrowed red velvet doublet.

'Keep it well hidden,' growled David in mock-concern. 'The Bordeaux tailor would drop dead if he knew what was lying next to his fine stitches.'

Martin grinned back. David thought that he looked stronger. His face was flushed pink and his eyes were much brighter.

'Dinna be feared. By dawn it'll be ten miles from here ... How hot this fire is!' He put his hand to his head. 'My brains are cracking.'

David tried to hide his concern. 'Then sit back, you gowk! Still, if you're going to sleep outside, you'd best make the most of the heat while you can.'

Martin had said he would return to the stable as soon as it was dark enough for him to slip out unseen. He did not want to risk anyone seeing him open Master Reid's door so late in the night, when he made for the Cupar road at midnight.

'It's no good,' said David to Elspeth, when she tried to persuade him to sleep in the house, 'he's as obstinate as the Devil.'

'Aye, that's right,' grinned Martin. They all knew how lame the reason was: the truth was that he wanted to cause them as little risk as possible, and intended to say he had come to the stable unasked if he was caught.

David took a blanket down to the stable and unhappily watched Martin settle down for the few hours before he began his journey.

'Are you sure you'll be warm enough? There's frost in the air.'

'Aye! I'm on fire – feel my hands! Just leave me some water. I've such a drouth on me. I canna mind when I ever drank so much.'

'Martin, I don't know when I shall go back to France. When I do, shall I send word to you at Lindores?'

Martin peered at him in the semi-darkness. 'You can try.' He groaned wearily. 'On your road, David, man. If I dinna take some rest now you'll find me still lying here in the morning.'

It was too dark to make out his expression. David told himself he was a fool to feel such anxiety. Martin sounded calm and knew how to look after himself on the walk to north Fife. He tried to keep himself awake, so that he would hear Martin going at midnight. But long before, he had fallen asleep and Mistress Binnie was raking the peat-ashes next day when he awoke.

He went down the garden path before breakfast, not too hurriedly, to collect the blanket. There was no one in sight, but it was as well to be careful. He heard a rustle in the straw of the stable, and picked up a stick to hit the rat that must be nesting there. But no rat made that kind of noise: a long, strangled moan that broke into grunts like someone heaving at a heavy block of stone.

Martin was tossing on the straw. He had thrown off the blanket and most of his clothes. His face was blotched and streaming with sweat, and his open mouth showed a black and swollen tongue. Although his eyes stared straight at David, he did not see him.

'Holy Mother!' David crossed himself. He ran towards Martin and then stepped back.

'Father Anthony,' he thought in a panic, 'I must find Father Anthony.'

The canon stood up and brushed the straw from the skirts of his black robe. 'He is delirious. Before evening he may have convulsions. After that, David, I am afraid there will be no hope for him.'

'There must be something you can do!'

'Oh, yes – spices in wine, angelica, theriac, clysters, bleeding – there are dozens of remedies. None of them much good. We don't know yet what causes this illness. If the boils can be fomented and broken, sometimes a man recovers.'

'Not Martin?'

Father Anthony gripped his shoulder. 'David, I'm sorry. You wouldn't thank me if I lied to you. Try to be calm. It is God's will. Leave him now.'

David's feet dragged up the garden path and he went to sit by the hearth with his head in his hands. The three others were there, but they did not speak to him. He was grateful for their silence, although he had come back to the house to report what the canon had said. When they talked it was in whispers to each other.

'Martin's dying and I've brought the plague among you,' he cried out. Master Reid went pale, but said nothing. Elspeth came and put a bowl of broth beside David.

'Come on,' she said, 'try to eat something. You've been fasting all day.' He shook his head and pushed it away.

Later in the day he took a pail of water down to the stable. Father Anthony had said the only relief he could give Martin was to keep his face cool and give him water to drink when he seemed to need it. He found the canon kneeling beside Martin with his hand on his forehead.

'He has a cold sweat,' he said to David. David stared dumbly at his friend. Suddenly the canon leant forward and lifted one of Martin's eyelids. 'You must leave us now, David, although I don't think he will be able to speak to me.'

'I'll stay! Do you think I'm afraid to see him die?'

The canon opened a leather case that David had not noticed before.

'No, David, I know you are not afraid. But we must be alone. I am not only his physician. I am his priest.'

They knew as soon as they heard the canon's footsteps outside the hall door. Master Reid and Elspeth crossed themselves, and Mistress Binnie rocked to and fro, weeping, as she moaned, 'The poor laddie! The poor laddie!'

The canon looked at them gravely. 'You know that every case of the pest in the town has to be reported.'

Master Reid pulled his beard. 'Who's to ken?' he asked jerkily, but dropped his eyes as the canon looked at him. 'No, Father, we canna ask you to have it on your conscience.'

Elspeth confronted Father Anthony. 'I canna take my grandmother to the pest-huts. She'd die of the cold!'

'There are thirty other women there, Elspeth, and some of them are as old as your grandmother.'

'I'll not do it!' she cried frantically. 'I'll go myself, but I'll not let you send her.'

The canon put his hands in the sleeves of his black robe and walked up and down the room. 'The pest is leaving us, thank God. It dies away in the winter months. The cold will be endurable if we have a good spring, and it will be only forty days.'

Elspeth's breast heaved with passion. 'I'll not, I'll not!' she screamed.

'Very well.' The canon stood in front of her. 'In England, they shut the houses up when someone is infected. Everyone stays inside them. *Everyone.* Do you understand? None of you can go out for forty days, not even into the garden. Food will be put out for you, but you must pull it up to the windows in baskets. You mustn't open the door, or the shutters, either, except when you pull up the food. I can't come in to you. There are many sick in the town, and if I come in, I shall have to be enclosed too ... Well?'

'I'll stay,' said Elspeth.

'All of you or none,' said the canon sternly. 'I know the bailies will not be satisfied with less. Henry Reid?'

The merchant sucked in his cheeks. 'Aye, Father, I'll stay.' The words could hardly be heard.

'David?'

'It's my fault,' said David, in a low voice. 'I'll do what the others want.'

The canon raised his hand and made the sign of the cross above their heads. Then he said, 'David, come with me. We have one more thing to do.'

They walked down the garden. The canon had already wrapped Martin's body in the blanket and now he lashed together four sticks to make a rough hurdle.

'We must go to the plague-pit by the Swilcan Burn.'

He put his lantern on the ground and the light fell on something half-hidden in the straw. As the canon stooped to pick up one end of the hurdle, with his back to him, David snatched up Martin's English Testament.

'Are you ready?' said Father Anthony over his shoulder. David lifted a corner of the blanket. He wedged the book under Martin's arm.

'Yes.' He bent to pick up the lantern and his own end of the hurdle.

The Swallow Port should have been locked, but the Castilians had long ago broken the gates and there was no porter now to guard the entry. They trudged through and past the site of the Regent's camp; the frost crackled under their feet, and they could hear the tide beating on the cliffs to their right.

'Is it far?' asked David.

'No. Can you see the lights of the pest-camp down there? The pit is about a hundred yards nearer the sea.'

The rough ground began to slope downwards to the sandy links. They could hear voices from the plague-huts and laughter and singing. David listened in amazement. How could people driven out of the town, waiting to die, be happy? He felt that he would never be without this cold ache inside him.

Five lanterns burned on the edge of the plague-pit. Father Anthony stooped near the edge and they set down their load. David gazed in revulsion at the white, glimmering depths, where piles of quick-lime hid the bodies.

'Do we –' He pointed downwards, feeling as if a hand squeezed his throat.

'Yes.' Father Anthony picked up a shovel by the pile of lime lying near the edge. 'Will you do it, please, David?'

David tipped one end of the hurdle. He held the blanket round Martin's body so that the English Testament should not fall away from him. He shut his eyes and jerked the poles. When he opened them Father Anthony was throwing the last spadeful of lime into the pit. David knelt beside him.

'I don't care if it is heresy,' he thought, listening to the Latin prayers. 'Martin wanted his Testament. Holy Mother, forgive me if I have sinned.'

When the canon had finished he said that he would visit the plague-camp before he returned to the Priory. David went back to Castle Wynd alone. The path to the top of the cliffs seemed steeper; he began to gasp for air and his breathing turned into a long shudder. He felt his forehead: the skin was cool, yet his hands were trembling, and his eyes began to fill with tears. He brushed them away, ashamed of his weakness, but they came back again. He managed to control himself as he went back through the Swallow Port and walked past the dark Castle walls.

There were lights in the chapel and he could hear the words of the hymn. He leant against the gate of the forecourt, as exhausted as if he had walked for several miles against a gale.

Go, heart, unto the lamp of light,
Go, heart, do service and honour.
Go, heart, and serve him day and night,
Go, heart, unto thy Saviour.

Go, heart, with true and full intent,
To Christ thy help and whole succour.
Thee to relieve he was all rent.
Go, heart, unto thy Saviour.

David stood there for a long time with the tears running down his face. Then he groped his way up Castle Wynd, thankful that there were no lights showing through the shutters of Master Reid's house. He bolted the door behind him and went to the fire to warm himself before going to bed. Without bothering to draw forward a stool he sat on the floor, huddling as far forward as he could, with his arms clasped round his knees. There was a movement in the shadow beside him.

'Elspeth,' he said, too weary to be surprised.

'Aye, I was waiting for you.' She wriggled forward and put an arm round him. David dropped his head on his knees.

'Do you hate me for bringing the plague here, Elspeth?'

He wanted some firm denial, but all she gave him was a quiet, 'No, David.'

Waves of misery flowed through him. He took Elspeth's hand. He began to talk about Martin: the arguments they had had in St Leonard's, the dog Aristotle, their games of golf, and what he had done with the English Testament. Elspeth listened in silence, even when he stopped talking for a moment. When he had been talking for half an hour or so, she was still watching his face, with his hand held tightly in both of hers.

'You are very kind, Cousin,' he said, and stopped, realizing what he had done. Elspeth smiled at him, but showed no surprise. He bent closer to her face to make sure the faint peat glow had not deceived him.

'You know!' he cried. 'How long have you known?'

'Since I saw your father's rings. My mother had one just the very same, till she had to sell it. I havena told my grandmother.'

Her words brought a quick rush of shame. 'Oh, Elspeth,' he muttered, turning his face away. He kicked at the peat ashes. 'When I get back to France I'll send such presents back to you! You'll never be poor or hungry again. Maybe you can visit us in Bordeaux.'

She put her hand to his cheek and slid it gently over his mouth. 'Wheesht, wheesht, keep all your fine promises for another forty days. Nobody kens what may come to us by then.'

His heart sank. He had almost forgotten. Forty days. They might all be dead by the beginning of April. He took Elspeth's face between his hands.

'Aren't you frightened?'

She smiled. 'I'm so feared I'd rather die now than bide to see what happens.'

David looked at her doubtfully. 'But you're smiling.' She did not answer and David's hands dropped to his knees.

'You're smiling yourself,' she said softly, and rose to her feet. 'I'm away to my bed. My grandmother may wake and be eerie if she finds herself alone. Good night, David.'

He was not sure if it was her hand or the edge of her sleeve that brushed his hair. He sat staring into the last glimmer of the peat, bewildered, because under his grief for Martin, and the cold grip of the plague-fear, a small warmth had begun to glow. He put his hand to his face, stiff and scorched from the heat of the fire, and he found that his mouth was still set in a smile.

CHAPTER FOURTEEN

Quarantine

FOR the first week they watched each other for signs of the plague. In the morning, when they met in the hall, they hung back a moment, to make sure. But on the seventh morning Elspeth did a surprising thing. After opening the door of her bedroom she ran to David with her eyes shut. She flung her arms around him.

'I wouldna keep away from you, even if you had it.' She opened her eyes to look at him.

He pushed her away gently and went on lacing his doublet. 'I'm still clean,' he reassured her, and wondered why she was so distressed.

Father Anthony brought their food at dawn. Later in the day two watchmen came with water and some peat or driftwood for the fire. They set all this under the window of the hall, and fastened it to the ropes that dangled from the sill. The shutters had to be kept bolted until the watchmen had retreated to the other side of the courtyard, where they stirred up the bonfire that was supposed to kill the poisonous vapours of the plague. They were allowed to tip their refuse out of another window overlooking the garden, once a day, but otherwise the shutters had to be bolted.

On the first morning David put his head out of the window as the watchman tied the rope to the pail. He looked up, covered his face, and shouted, 'Hold your head in, laddie, or I'll let you starve!'

They still had five sacks of the Regent's flour under the

bed, so they would not go without food. But they were short of water and fuel. The two pailfuls they were allowed cooked their meals and gave them water to drink, but nothing more. Their clothes and bodies grew filthy, but they were too afraid of the plague to mind the dirt.

Master Reid wanted to give the watchmen presents. He wrapped an ivory crucifix and his silver-gilt salt-cellar in a napkin, and tied the bundle to the rope-end. When Elspeth asked what he was doing he said, 'They brought us only three bits of peat yesterday and the salt fish had maggots in it.'

'If they'll not do their best for charity, have you enough to bribe them for forty days?'

He blinked, and then nodded his head. 'Aye, you're right. It was a wastrife thing to do.' He returned the crucifix and salt-cellar to their cupboard.

The days were dreary and cold as they huddled round the small peat fire. 'Now I know why they had to sing in the plague-camp,' David told himself, as the afternoons stretched endlessly to darkness and sleep. While the light lasted – and they were always in half-darkness, because the lower half of each window was darkened by the bolted shutters – Master Reid fidgeted from one room to the other, making an inventory of everything in his chests and linen-presses. When he could find no more to check, he sat by the fire twisting his fingers. He did the same thing every day.

He gave some of his dead wife's gowns to Elspeth, and she unpicked and renewed them for her grandmother and herself. She asked David what the fashions were in France.

'Does it matter?' he asked. Elspeth went on unpicking the blue woollen cloth for a moment, and then she said, 'Not if we live through the quarantine. If we're all to die,

I'll bear it better with some work in my hands.' And David felt ashamed of his despair.

But it was hard to live through the monotonous, idle days. He told them about the young Florentines, who had shut themselves up to escape the plague two hundred years before, and passed the time in telling each other stories. He repeated as many as he could remember, but Mistress Binnie kept interrupting with questions, until they all forgot what the story was about. So for the first time since he had left the *Giroflée*, he picked up his lute. He played and sang for them, French songs, and some of the Scots songs his mother had taken to Bordeaux.

'I ken that tune,' said Elspeth suddenly one evening. 'My own mother used to sing it. It's about the wife of Auchtermuchty that went to yoke the plough-oxen, and told her man to bide at home and mind the bairns. It's well-kent round the Lomonds.' They smiled at each other, remembering their family. They had told no one else their secret.

'Let's see if we can mind on the words,' said Elspeth. They spent two happy hours prompting and contradicting each other, while Master Reid stared gloomily from the other side of the hearth.

It was a game that lasted only one evening. Master Reid shut himself in his own room; he said that he was going to pray, but they felt he was bored with the songs and stories that they all had heard too many times. David remembered his Greek books. They were at the bottom of the chest that had been sent back to St Andrews in the *Giroflée* in November. He took out his Odyssey and read aloud.

'I ken better charms than you,' said Mistress Binnie contemptuously. Elspeth silenced her grandmother and, for a short time, listened to the lilting, incomprehensible hexameters. Then she, too, became bored. David tried to read silently, but his pleasure had gone. He shut the book and gazed into the fire in numb despair.

After he had spent two days sitting in silence, or walking restlessly from one window to the other, Elspeth said reprovingly, 'You'll weary yourself to death long before the pest catches you.'

David scratched at a knot in the table with his dagger. 'What can I do?'

'You were gey anxious for your books down at the harbour.'

'And now we haven't even the nets to mend.'

Elspeth hid her face over her sewing. 'Maybe you could teach me my letters.'

Master Reid looked up. 'That's a daft notion, Elspeth. What call has a lassie like you to read? My Katharine couldna spell her own name.'

'I'd like fine to learn.'

David's lips tightened as Master Reid clucked in disapproval. He pulled a charred stick from the fire and cleared a space among the ashes. On the stone hearth he scrawled five letters.

'A, B, C, D, and E to stand for "Elspeth". See if you can copy them.' He held her hand on the stick to guide her. Master Reid bent forward jealously.

'Good sakes, look at all yon French curlicues! Can you not teach her a plain Scots hand? Here, give me the stick.'

They spent the rest of the day quarrelling over the right way to teach Elspeth the alphabet. They stopped for dinner and in the afternoon began again. By the time there was no light but the peat glow, they had taught her to write her own name and four other letters.

The next day before breakfast Master Reid trimmed

a quill pen and offered Elspeth an ink-pot and a page in his account-book. 'If the lassie has to write her name, here's a better way to do it.'

David glowered and held out the pewter ink-pot. 'Go on, Elspeth, it's easy.'

Elspeth turned the quill in her fingers. 'I'm feared I'll smirch it.' She dabbed at the paper nervously with the horny tip of the pen, and in crooked, sprawling letters wrote 'Elspeth Binnie'.

'There,' she said, and her eyes sparkled.

Master Reid took the pen from her. Underneath he wrote, 'The fifteenth day of March, A.D. 1547.' He signed his own name below and drew a large flourish to enclose the two names.

'There,' he echoed, sounding very pleased.

Anger blurred David's eyes. His hands trembled and he pressed them tightly under his belt. Elspeth spoke. He had to ask her to repeat the words.

'Guide my hand, David. I'd like fine to write your name beside ours.'

His fingers locked with hers over the quill. She looked at him quickly and he relaxed his grip. On the opposite page, in letters twice as large as Master Reid's, he made Elspeth write, 'David Lindsay'.

He watched her face as they wrote the words together, and his anger changed to astonishment at the strange thing that was happening inside him. Elspeth's hands, like his own, were grimy and black-nailed. The foul air in the shuttered rooms had made their unwashed bodies smell like foxes. Yet for the first time he found that Elspeth was beautiful; he longed to touch her neck and dark hair, so close to his face.

'I love her,' he thought to himself. He was bewildered.

Surely love was something to do with Italian sonnets, and fine clothes, and kissing Marie of Bordeaux in the rose-garden, when her mother wasn't looking?

He waited until the old woman was dozing over the fire and Master Reid had gone once more to check his linen.

'Elspeth,' he whispered, 'I have something to tell you.'

'No, David, dinna say it!' She looked more agitated than he had ever seen her. 'Not just now. Wait until the quarantine's over.'

'Why?'

She looked down and reddened. 'Maybe you'd be vexed at yourself later.' She laughed awkwardly. 'Folk take strange notions when they're shut up.' She pressed his hand and slipped away to the next room.

David frowned, trying to understand. Marie of Bordeaux would have blushed and drawn him on. Elspeth was a child compared with artful Marie; yet in some ways she seemed a hundred years older.

The morning after Elspeth wrote her name in the account-book, a young Franciscan brought their food. David pushed open the shutter, forgetting the quarantine rules. 'Where is Father Anthony?'

The friar was already walking away. 'He is ill,' he called over his shoulder.

'Is it the plague?' But the young Franciscan had already gone round the corner.

No one came near the house except the watchmen. David wrote a letter to the canon and threw it down on the cobbles. One of the men picked it up on his staff-end and without reading it threw it into the fire that burned in the middle of the court-yard.

'Dinna do that again!' he shouted. 'It's against the regulations.'

They talked about it for a time and tried to convince themselves that Father Anthony had some slight illness. But he did not come to them during the rest of their quarantine.

A few days after the Franciscan began to bring their food, Master Reid said that there were several men in Castle Wynd, watching the house. Richard Strang was with them. David went to the gable-end window and looked up the street. The men were talking quietly; each of them had a cudgel tucked into his belt.

'They're feared to come near because of the pest,' said Master Reid behind him. 'Look at them. Just shiftless gangrels and a few of the younkers. They'd never dare stravaig around like this if it werena for the Castilians and the pest. Dinna let on to the women folk, Davy.'

The men began to gather outside every morning. Each day they came nearer, until they stood in the courtyard under the windows of the hall. At the end of a week they were standing quite near the forestair, and called out two words in time to the beating of a small drum. There were fifteen or twenty of them.

'What's yon noise?' asked Mistress Binnie.

The voices rose. 'Henry Reid! Henry Reid!' they chanted. David saw the watchmen try to drive the men away with their white-tipped sticks. Master Reid peered through the dark glass of the upper window.

'Henry Reid! Henry Reid!'

Master Reid's hands shook as he unbolted the shutters. 'What do you want, you limmers?' he roared. David looked over his shoulder and saw Richard Strang beating the town drum. The apprentice waved his drum-sticks and the words changed.

'Send the old wife to the pest-camp! Send the old wife to the pest-camp!'

Master Reid drew in his head and bolted the shutters again. Of the other two, only Elspeth had heard the words. She took her grandmother to the window that overlooked the garden, pretending that she wanted to fit a sleeve on her arm. The old woman shook her head indignantly. 'Ill-guided loons! What are they saying?'

'Stupid blethers. They're only prentice-lads, roaming the town.'

The noise went on all morning. At noon the crowd dispersed, but the men came back again later. On the second day a handful of pebbles spattered against the courtyard window. For a moment there was a sudden silence; then the men scrambled over the rubble of the cooper's house, looking for more stones. The watchmen shouted at them, but ran away as the stones were thrown at the window. The thick green glass tinkled on the floor of the hall.

Master Reid cried furiously, 'I'll have them in the burgh court! I'll have them whipped at the cart-tail and put in the jougs for a week!'

David and Elspeth pulled a bench across the broken window. 'David, are they going to break in?' she asked.

'I don't know.' He began to drag an oak chest towards the front door. But the shouts and rattling of stones abruptly stopped. There was a clatter of hooves in the street and the sound of running footsteps. David looked through one of the cracked panes. The courtyard was empty. At its far end, over the smoke of the bonfire, he saw a troop of mounted Castilians trotting up the street.

In a few moments Castle Wynd was silent. The watchmen came out of their hiding-places and stood by the bonfire again.

As the remaining days of their imprisonment dragged by they began to hope that the plague had missed them.

The cold air eased itself between the rags they had stuffed in the broken panes. Although they shivered, they welcomed its icy freshness in the foul rooms, and thought it smelt of spring. But almost every night a light, sleety rain fell on the town. It seeped through the cracks, and the inside walls became furred with a green dampness.

'At least the rain holds them off at night,' said Elspeth. 'We can sleep at night.'

On the thirty-ninth day of their quarantine, David wrote a sentence for Elspeth to copy. 'Easter will set us free. Lord Jesus preserve us. Amen.'

On the fortieth morning they threw open all the shutters and unbarred the door. The watchmen were quenching the bonfire with pailfuls of water.

'I can smell the sea!' cried Elspeth in delight. 'I'll clean all the rooms and burn sweet herbs on the fire.'

Mistress Binnie shuffled to the door and stood like a bulky night-bird blinking in the sunshine. 'Eh, sirs, I can hear the bells.' They listened and between the peals from the Cathedral and Holy Trinity Kirk, David thought he could hear Elizabeth, the bell of St Leonard's.

'It's Easter Sunday,' said Master Reid. 'We must go to mass.'

Round the corner of the house came Father Anthony. They went down the forestair to meet him, and he stood in the courtyard, holding out his hands. He smiled, but he looked thinner. His face was haggard and almost as white as his tonsured hair.

'Yes, I am well,' he assured them. 'It was only a fever and not the plague, praise God.' But David saw the canon sway on his feet and brought him a stool from the hall.

'Tell us the news,' begged Elspeth.

'There are still thirty poor souls in the plague-camp, but no more sick in the town for a whole week. The

Castilians have sent their preachers to turn the townsfolk against the priests. They argue with the University men and the sub-Prior in Holy Trinity.'

'Bonny preachers on horseback!' spat Mistress Binnie.

'You must have seen the horsemen paid by the English Protector. The English King has died, and the French King, too. But the English are still helping Norman Leslie. His Holiness has sent the remission for the Castilians – that's why we're saying mass again. The Castilians won't accept it. So the Queen Dowager has sent to France for help. Perhaps she'll be sent guns and ships by the new King.'

David exclaimed, 'Won't the Regent attack the Castle again?'

Father Anthony shrugged. 'He plans to take an army to the English border in the summer.' He began to cough and the colour came and went in his face. David watched him anxiously.

Master Reid listened impatiently to all this public news. 'Who's dead in the town?' The canon gave him a list of names, and at the end he said, 'James Brown, Deacon of the Bakers, has died of the plague.'

Master Reid looked stricken as he crossed himself. 'Jamie Brown! What about that poor soul, his wife?'

'Madge had to go to the plague-camp. If she lives she can go home next week, if her house is safe till then. The Castilians broke into the cellars yesterday and took away all her blankets, and three kitchen cauldrons.'

'I'll cry in and see if I can keep the door locked,' said Master Reid.

The canon stood up slowly. 'I must go now and find some food for the plague-camp. There's no one else to take it now that James Brown is dead.'

They watched him go away and looked at each other.

'Och well,' said Master Reid uncomfortably, 'we must be on our road to Holy Trinity. Elspeth, my doo, put on that new blue kirtle. We must pray for Father Anthony's good health.'

'Not just pray,' said David under his breath. As they walked through the streets to the church, he wondered what Elspeth would say when she heard what he was going to do.

CHAPTER FIFTEEN

'The Old Wife Brought the Pest'

'ARE you glaikit, Davy?' cried Master Reid. 'God has saved us, and you want to go down to the pest-camp! It's not right to put us in danger again.'

David tried to tell him again: the people in the camp were not plague-struck, but only waiting for the end of their quarantine. 'Father Anthony is ill. He needs my help. Have you no pity for them?'

Master Reid tugged his beard. 'Aye, poor souls ... but I'll not eat with you. You can sleep in my room and go in and out by the ladder. We'll put your food by the door. I'll sleep in the hall.'

David turned to Elspeth. She said uncertainly, 'I dinna want you to go, but I think you must.'

David ran down the forestair seething with angry contempt against Master Reid. Elspeth came after him.

'Dinna get into a blaze, David. He canna help it. He's more feared of the pest than you are.'

David glared. 'He might as well ask me to leave the house.'

'But he *didna*! I canna bear to see the two of you cast out. Be easy with him, David. And take care of yourself.'

Her distress shamed him into a better humour. 'You needna fash yourself,' he teased her. 'I'll not give you the pest.'

She smiled faintly at his imitation of her Fife accent.

'That's not it. It's you I'm feared for.'

When he met the canon, David walked as slowly as he

could; but Father Anthony was impatient with his own weakness and kept on urging him to hurry.

'We must go to Southgate first. I may be given some food for them there.'

They called at some of the merchants' stone houses and received six stale loaves, the scourings of a barrel of salted pork, and a few dried plums. Father Anthony put all these into a canvas bag. It was light, but he did not protest when David took it from him.

David wondered why the Priory kitchens could not spare some food for the plague-camp. He had not the courage to ask Father Anthony, and he grumbled about the smallness of the merchants' gifts instead.

'They haven't much food themselves,' said the canon, and David remembered the sacks of flour still hidden under Master Reid's bed. He flushed and said no more.

They walked along the top of the cliffs. A strong wind blew the spray off the sea, but the waves were curling torrents of blue, and the sky glittered with cold sunshine. North of the bay, the Grampian peaks were tipped with white, looking tiny but near, like the hills in his father's missal. David whistled under his breath as the salty air stung his cheeks.

The canon smiled. 'Your face will be the best medicine for my patients.'

But no one in the plague-camp was outside to enjoy the fine morning. The vast sprawl of huts by the Swilcan Burn was half empty now. There were only ten where the smoke still eddied through the reed thatching.

In the first hut an old man lay alone. Father Anthony lifted him and fed him with bread and water. He bent forward to catch the old man's cracked whisper. 'He says there are no more sick today. Praise God. The plague is going.'

They went round the other huts. The people inside were weak with hunger, and their eyes were bloodshot because of the everlasting reek of their fires. Firewood, gathered mostly from the West Sands, was the one thing they had in abundance.

David helped the canon to divide the food and feed the oldest and youngest, who were too lethargic to lift it to their mouths, even when it was broken and dipped in water for them.

A tight, indignant lump pressed round David's heart. 'How can the bailies leave them like this? It's wicked!'

'No, not wicked. Most of the bailies are dead. The townsfolk are afraid to come here. They would help if they knew how. They have no one to lead them.'

Most of the huts held two or three people. In the last they entered there was a thin, elderly woman. Ash was engrained in her skin, and her grey hair straggled from under a filthy coif. 'Have you brought me a fine mutton-pie, Father?' she joked, and held out her grimy hand. The canon gave her the last piece of salted pork. 'More rind than anything,' she grumbled, 'but it's nourishment.' Her eyes were bright with grim humour as she tore the pork with her teeth.

With amazement David recognized Madge Brown, the widow of the Deacon of the Bakers. He remembered her handing the canon a bag of oatmeal – plump, bold-faced, wearing a spotless kirtle and fine linen.

Widow Brown stared back at him. 'You're the laddie that came to see my man when he had the sore leg. You're one of the St Leonard's clerks.'

David nodded. He wondered if James Brown had died in this hut. Widow Brown wiped her mouth and sat back on the pile of straw and ragged blankets. 'And are you still swithering? Do you still no ken if you're to be a doctor?'

David smiled at her rough, teasing voice. He began to make a joking answer, but his tongue faltered and his heart began to hammer with excitement. When the confusion went, it left something plain and simple in his mind. He realized that it had been there for a long time.

'Yes,' he said. 'I've decided to become a doctor. I'll begin to study when I go back to France.'

The canon was smiling at him.

When he returned to Master Reid's house, David began to climb the ladder fixed to the gable. Master Reid looked out of the window above. 'Go round to the door,' he said gruffly.

Inside the hall he muttered, 'I'm sorry, Davy,' and pointed to the table where Elspeth and Mistress Binnie were waiting to start their meal. Elspeth looked elated; David wondered whether she had coaxed or bullied Master Reid out of his panic.

'I've seen Mistress Brown in the plague-camp,' he said, when they had eaten. 'She needs food. They all do.'

'Poor souls,' said Master Reid, with a sigh.

'We have plenty of flour.'

Elspeth cried, 'We could bake for them!'

'Not so fast!' said Master Reid nervously.

David checked his impatience. 'You needn't bake as much bread as you did for the court. And I could take it down to the camp.'

Master Reid twisted his beard. 'What if Richard Strang and the others heard about it?'

'They're starving. The maggots will be at that flour before we can eat it all ourselves.'

'Let's help them, Harry,' begged Elspeth.

'It would be a Christian-like thing to do,' said Master Reid doubtfully. 'Maybe they'll not find out ... Well, what if they did? They couldna hate me worse. And it would please Father Anthony. Aye, my bairns, we'll do it!' He banged the table enthusiastically. 'We'll bake the first batch tomorrow forenoon!'

For a few days no one seemed to notice that Master Reid's oven had been fired again. Then the new Deacon, a much younger man than James Brown, called at the house. After their interview Master Reid was silent and anxious-faced, but he would not say what had happened.

'Perhaps we ought to stop baking,' said David, hoping that Elspeth would contradict him.

'It's only another few days,' she said indignantly. 'We said we'd feed them till they go home. We canna go back on our promise.'

So David forgot his uneasiness and continued to take the bread down to the plague-camp. There were no more demonstrations outside the house. He convinced himself that he had been too anxious; possibly Master Reid had been told he would have to pay some huge amount of money to be re-enrolled among the city bakers.

One evening David returned very late to the house. After visiting the plague-camp he had walked round the town looking for someone who could take a message to Martin's mother. At last, in one of the ale-houses, he found a pedlar who often took the route between St Andrews and Lindores. He gave the man a letter to take to the almoner at Lindores Abbey, asking him to pass the news on to Martin's mother.

As he hurried home, still thinking about Martin, he saw a bonfire lighted by the Mercat Cross. 'That's strange,' he thought. It was some distance from the unclean houses. The men crowding round it were not Castilians, yet many of them carried whingers and short pikes.

When they were eating supper a pebble rattled against the window.

'Leave it be,' said Master Reid. 'An honest neighbour would chap at the door.'

After a short silence more pebbles were thrown. Master Reid hesitated and then made a signal to David. He half-opened the shutter and thought he could see someone standing below.

'I've come for Elspeth,' a voice whispered.

'Who the devil are you?'

'Richard Strang. Tell her Wat Edie and his billies are on the road here. I'll take her to my mother's house by the West Port. I've left Deacon Brown's.'

Elspeth's curiosity brought her to join David at the window. She thrust her head outside and spoke at the top of her voice. 'Rap off, Richard Strang. D'you think I'd trust myself to *you*?'

The whisper became urgent. 'They're coming here with torches. Come away, Elspeth!'

She spread her elbows on the sill. 'You set them on. Canna you hold them in?'

The figure pleaded, 'Dinna cry so loud! They say the old wife brought the pest into the town when she touched the pikeman. They're on the road to stop you baking. Elspeth, I dinna want to see you harmed.'

'Tell him to link off,' screeched Mistress Binnie from the hearth. But Elspeth hung out of the window calling down abuse at Richard Strang, and putting into it all the irritation and fears of the past six weeks.

'Leave him alone,' said David. 'The cold will soon drive him away.' He tried to pull Elspeth back; they were pushed aside as Mistress Binnie buffeted her way between them. They jumped back as they saw the smouldering peat she carried in a pair of tongs.

'Take that, you loon,' she screamed, dropping the peat out of the window. 'And the fire of Hell in your bones as well!' She chuckled breathlessly.

Richard Strang yelped and seemed to have fallen on the cobbles. The hot turf sent out a shower of sparks, and then glowed dully on the ground. The white blur of Strang's face turned up to them in the darkness. 'You'll be the one to burn, you old witch! You and your whole clamjamfrey!'

As he vanished, Master Reid drew the old woman from the window and began to pile furniture against the door. He brought out some candle-stumps that had been carefully saved through their quarantine. He lit them with shaking fingers.

'We'd best see what we're about.' His face was as green as it had been the morning after the storm, in the *Giroflée*.

The candles had guttered to pools of smoking tallow before they heard what they expected. At first it seemed part of the noise of waves against the cliffs; then it turned into the tramp of feet and a rising babble of voices. Castle Wynd was empty, but they could see close-packed lines of men, many holding torches, advancing across the cooper's garden.

'Holy Mother,' said Master Reid, 'they mean to set us on fire!'

The lights came forward, until they could see the faces and shoulders of the crowd. The men shouted and waved their torches. The dancing light made them look like a vast army as they surrounded the garden side of the house. A few yards from the curving wall of the bakehouse oven, they halted.

Elspeth clung to David's arm and pressed her head into his shoulder. 'David, I'm feared,' she whispered.

He held her tightly. Master Reid came to stand behind them.

'You needna bide here,' he said. 'It's me they're after, because of the baking. Maybe the old wife as well. You could try to take her out by the door.'

'We're biding with you. All of us,' said Elspeth.

Master Reid put an arm round each of them. 'Very well, my bairns.' By the hearth Mistress Binnie was muttering to herself. She seemed to have gone into one of her senseless moods. She rocked to and fro by the fire, crooning to herself as she twisted a ragged thread of wool off the dead Mistress Reid's distaff. The noise had turned into uproar outside, but she did not seem to hear it.

David said, 'At least we can see them. It's not like waiting for the plague.'

'Aye, Davy, but I wish I had put my new slate roof on the rigging before they killed the Cardinal. My thatch will soon be in a blaze.'

Elspeth gasped. The shouts grew louder, and the men brandished their torches like fiery spears. But they were not moving closer.

'It only needs the one of them to start,' said Master Reid. His voice rose hopefully. 'Maybe they'll not have the smeddum to do it.'

Elspeth ran to the courtyard window. Presently she cried, 'There's six of them by the forestair. They're casting their torches at the thatch!'

Master Reid went to see. 'We'll roast like Christmas apples. Maybe I should go out to them.'

David asked if he had a firehook. 'Aye, fastened to the gable beside the ladder. But what's the use?'

David went to the end room and leant out of the window. He twisted round to look at the roof; dimly, he could see the ladder running up towards the thatch, and the long pole tipped with an iron claw hooked to the wall beside it. The firebrands hissed over the roof-top above him, but this gable-end of the house was in darkness. With luck, no one would see him.

He was standing on the window-sill with one foot groping for the ladder, when he heard Elspeth whisper behind him, 'David, dinna climb up there, my dear.'

He bent towards her and touched her shoulder. For one moment he pulled her into his arms. They could go down the ladder, he thought. They would soon escape in the darkness. He hesitated. Then he swung himself out on the ladder. 'I won't be long,' he said, and grasped the fire-hook.

It was easy enough to climb the ladder, but almost impossible to scramble on to the roof while he was holding the twenty-foot pole. In the end he lashed the pole with his belt to the upper part of the ladder, climbed on to the thatch and leant over to tug the pole free. He laid it flat by his left leg, and sat astride the roof-tree and wriggled towards the stone chimney-stack above the hall.

He knew the rioters would throw even more firebrands at the thatch if they saw him: a human target would make their sport more exciting. But he hoped that when he reached the shelter of the chimney-stack he could push the firebrands off with his pole.

Below him, the flame-lit figures jostled and shouted like the crowd at a summer fair. They had worked off their first anger, and they sounded boastful and cheerful. They took turns to hurl their torches at the roof and stamped and clapped each throw.

For some time the torches rolled back into the courtyard or garden. The resinous smoke made David cough, and as he swung his pole to sweep the first firebrand from the thatch, the crowd saw him.

A dozen men surged forward with a great shout and called for more faggots. As they threw them, David set his back to the chimney and shortened his grip on the pole. Thank God that a blazing piece of wood was hard to aim, he thought, as he held up one arm to protect his face. He was more bruised than burnt, and they seemed to be running short of missiles.

He realized soon that there was a stronger smell of burning near him. Another group must have attacked the gable-end, where tiny spurts edged the roof. He scrambled on hands and knees along the slippery thatch, once avoiding a fall by throwing himself, jack-knifed, across the roof-ridge. He had forgotten the pole, but it would have been useless here. He pulled his duelling dagger from his belt; he sawed the burning straw and jerked out the blazing tufts with his left hand.

There was a crackling sound behind him; across his shoulder David saw a flame creeping along the roof-ridge. He tore desperately at the thatch, and it seemed as if a thousand needles were being driven through his fingers. He pulled off his doublet to smother the flames. For a moment that worked, until the cloth smouldered and burned.

And then out of the sky came a stinging dampness. David lifted his face to the darkness and felt rain. At first it was a drizzle that made the tiny flames hiss more loudly; then came a sighing rush of wind, and the water poured down. The flames in the thatch guttered like dead candles; down in the garden the torches wavered and went out.

David laughed and held up his burnt hands to the sky. He shouted at the invisible rain: heathen gods' and saints' names and lurid tavern oaths were all jumbled into cracked, hysterical phrases, as he shouted with relief. Soon he was sodden to the skin and the thatch ran with water. No more flame could touch it that night.

He crawled back to the ladder, wincing as his weight fell on his scorched palms and fingers. He dropped to the cobbles and pressed his back against the wall. As he slid round the corner of the house, through the rain, David saw a glimmer of lanterns at the top of Castle Wynd. There was a great deal of noise with them, bumps and scraping sounds as if a farm-sledge was being dragged along the street.

As David ran to the forestair the breath was knocked out of him.

'Mind your feet, you clumsy stot!' roared the man he had run into, and he realized that the courtyard was full. The shouts began again as the sledge was hauled round the corner. Some of the men gathered on the forestair and others hammered at the door of the bakehouse.

'If I go up the forestair they'll follow and burst into the house,' he thought. By the blurred lantern-light he saw that the sledge was heaped with dung and midden-rubbish. The smell made him retch even in the rain-drenched air. He was swept by the mob against the wall and then through the bakehouse door as they wrenched it open.

Someone lit the rushlights and oil-crusies hanging on the walls. They kicked over the kneading-trough and began to shovel the manure into the oven, using the long wooden bread-peel and the water-buckets.

'Bring him down to watch!' yelled someone. Soon, above the uproar, David heard a splintering crash, as if the front door had been broken. They brought Master Reid, struggling and red-faced, into the bakehouse and stood him against the wall.

'Bake this bread for your pest-camp,' jeered Richard Strang, and flung a bucketful of filth over his former master. David fought against the press of bodies, but he could not reach Master Reid.

The noise died suddenly and silence spread to the far side of the bakehouse. Everyone turned to stare at the door. Mistress Binnie stood there, shaking with rage, her open mouth dribbling as she tried to speak. The men stepped away from her.

'You loons,' she screamed, 'get out, or I'll send a fiery rain on the pack of you! I'll make your womenfolk bear apes and chickens! Get out! I'll wither the heart in everyone I touch!'

She spread her fingers and clawed the air as she tottered towards them. The men nearest her backed away and someone at a safe distance yelled, 'Grip the old wife and cast her into the sea! She brought the pest to the town.'

'Into the sea?' shrieked Mistress Binnie. She pulled a rushlight from the wall and threw it at the crowd. 'It's cooler than the place you're going to, Wat Edie!'

David tried to reach her. If she recognized the man, perhaps she still had enough sense to let him take her away. But he was too late. The crowd surged forward and twenty hands grabbed her.

'Put the witch on the sledge!' They dragged it outside and placed her on it. Six men hauled on the ropes and a dozen more, some with lanterns, crowded round it to stop her getting off. They began to pull her down the street. David followed, vainly tugging at the arms and clothes of the men who marched beside the sledge. In the lantern-light Mistress Binnie teetered round and round on her slippery moving platform, screaming now with fear, not rage. They laughed and beat her back with their cudgels, and David stumbled behind, though the men struck at him more savagely now as he tried to pull them away from the sledge.

They had not far to go. They turned the corner of Castle Wynd and marched towards Kirk Hill. When they were clear of the Castle ramparts they dragged the sledge towards the cliffs. They thronged round it until they had taken it to the very edge of the rock. Then a dozen men bent down and David heard Richard Strang's excited shout:

'One, two, three, heave away, lads, and out!'

The others held up their lanterns and cheered. The sledge shot forward and with one last scream from Mistress Binnie it disappeared over the edge of the cliff.

CHAPTER SIXTEEN

A Ship for France

FOR three days Elspeth shut herself into the middle room and would not speak to either of them. Sometimes her hand came through to snatch the food they put beside the door, but she hardly touched it.

'It's not natural,' said Master Reid unhappily to David. 'When my poor Katharine lost our bairn she had half the women from the street beside her.'

'Elspeth's not like that,' said David. 'We must leave her alone.'

Father Anthony spoke to her through the door. At first she answered him in fierce, short sentences. Then she refused to speak, and he, too, said they must let her choose her own time.

They had searched for the body at the foot of the cliffs. On the rocks they found the broken sledge, but the body had been carried out to sea.

'Maybe we should walk round the cliffs towards Fife Ness,' suggested Master Reid.

David remembered the dead seal that he and Elspeth had found on the rocks. 'No. It will be better not to.'

They heard that Richard Strang had left the town for good. The streets were empty except for the forty Castilians riding by twice a day. The rioters did not come back to the house. David set about cleaning the oven and bakehouse. It was a disgusting task; but he was glad to have his mind taken off what had happened.

On the fourth morning Elspeth came into the hall. Her

face was white, with dark stains under the eyes. The two men looked at her silently.

'I'm going away. I canna bide here.'

Master Reid fussed round her, trying to make her sit down. She pushed him away and screamed at David, 'Well, you needna look so upset!'

'Elspeth,' pleaded Master Reid, 'we canna do without you.'

'Where will you go?' asked David. She shook her head and Master Reid plucked at her kirtle. 'You've got to earn your bread, lassie. Dinna be daft. Stay here.'

She turned on him fiercely. 'How can I, all on my lone? I'm sixteen now, and you're two men, and not another woman in the house.'

'What, after the way we've lived these past six weeks!' thought David incredulously. But he saw that Elspeth could bear no more. It would be unkind to argue with her.

'If you must go,' said Master Reid, 'go to Widow Brown. Her man the Deacon's dead, and the prentice ran away, and I ken the two servant-lassies died in the plague. She needs help in the house. She'll gladly give you your meat and fee.'

'Shall I do that, David?'

'Yes! I'll take you to her house.'

'Ask her if she'll give us our dinner,' said Master Reid. 'We'll pay her well.'

A wavering smile passed over Elspeth's face. 'Dinna fear, you'll not go without your meat. If she'll not dress it for you I'll come here at noon and do it myself.'

Master Reid looked relieved. When Elspeth went to her bedroom to tie a few clothes in a bundle, he sat down shaking his head, and muttered, 'What's got into the lassie,

Davy? I dinna understand at all. Her grannie's dead. She canna bring her back.'

David was numb with misery at the thought of Elspeth's departure. As she returned to the hall he took the bundle from her, and said in a stifled voice, 'Won't you change your mind?'

'No. It'll be better for us if I go.'

Master Reid walked across the room to open the hall door, but hesitated in front of it. 'You dinna have to go,' he burst out. 'You said you're sixteen, Elspeth. You're old enough to by my wife.' He stopped, looking frightened. David's heart seemed to slip sideways and Elspeth halted a few feet from the door. Then she came to put her hand on Master Reid's shoulder.

'Thank you, Harry. I couldna do it yet, could I? But I'll set my mind to it. Ask me again at the end of June.'

Henry Reid nodded as if he did not trust himself to speak, and held open the door. David followed Elspeth down the forestair, choking with grief and anger. Elspeth walked slowly. She seemed neither very surprised nor excited by the offer of marriage.

As they turned into Marketgate, where the Deacon's house stood, David could contain himself no longer. 'Elspeth, you can't! He's thirty years older than you!'

She lifted her eyebrows. 'That makes no odds. He's a kind man. He'll guide me well and maybe I'll bring a son. He'd like that.'

'You don't love him!'

'*Love?* David, do you think I'm one of those fine Italian ladies in the stories you told us? I've no kinsfolk now and my father was a fisherman. It would be a good marriage for me. And I am fond of him.'

'Your mother was a Lindsay of Pitcairnie.'

'Aye, and many a time she told me how she loved my father – but it didna stop her missing all the gentry ways and fine food at her old home. Forbye, why should I not love him?'

David was silent, so she said, more kindly, 'Well, what would you like me to do? Be practical!'

David put down her bundle outside the Tolbooth, where they now were, and seized her hands. 'Come back to France with me. We could travel to Leith and find a ship there, and sail to Bordeaux.'

She looked at him sadly for a few moments, while David thought, 'I said all that to Martin and it didn't happen.'

'What about your family, David? Would they want me?'

'My father would look after you. You can live with us.'

'And *then*?'

David grasped her hands more tightly. 'Elspeth, if you're old enough to marry Henry Reid, you're old enough to marry me. We could get a dispensation.'

She pulled her hands away. '*You* are not old enough to marry *me*.'

'I was seventeen at Christmas. I'll have to study for years. I'll be old enough then. I'm going to be a surgeon, like Ambroise Paré. We would have to wait, but you could have my sisters for your friends ... We'd see each other often.'

Elspeth turned her head away and David said despairingly, 'You don't want to come with me, do you?'

'It's all daftness. If I didna love you I'd make a gowk of you, and say I'd come. Of course I want to! But you ken fine you have to do what your father says till you finish your studies. You canna take me back to Bordeaux and tell your father to feed me, just because I'm your cousin ... Oh, I suppose he'd not turn me out on the streets! But

I canna come. I'd only bring you trouble, David. Let me alone.'

He wanted to rage and mock her dull common sense. But he knew she was right. It was his own fault. If only he had not tried so hard to save his pride. Last November he had begged his father not to let the Binnies know he was their cousin. He had wanted to repay them without telling them this one thing. Now it was too late. If he sent another letter, there would be no answer before Elspeth had married Master Reid. And he could not ask her to wait.

Elspeth was crying. David picked up her bundle and strode ahead of her, not looking back in case he spoke the useless, angry words that flooded his tongue. Outside Widow Brown's door he muttered, 'At least we can see each other before I go?'

'Of course. Dinna you mind that you're to come here for your dinner every day?'

When he returned home Master Reid was walking restlessly about the house. A woman's green woollen girdle dangled from his left hand. 'She's left a few things behind.' He did not meet David's eye. 'It'll be gey and dreich without her, Davy.'

They sat on opposite sides of the fire and Master Reid shuffled his heels in the ash. 'There's nothing to hinder you going now. I canna keep you to your promise now the womenfolk have gone.'

David looked round the room. It had never seemed so empty. 'What will you do?'

'Me? The steer will all die down now the old wife's dead.'

They sat in silence for a moment, then Master Reid went on, 'Father Anthony cried in while you were out with Elspeth. He said a messenger came from Edinburgh today. The French king has promised to help the Queen. He's to send a fleet of ships to take the Castle. So I'll be fine.'

'How will that help you?'

'They've had their sport with me, Davy. A year from now, and all the young bakers and prentices will be tipping their caps to the Provost in the street, all douce and quiet. I'll go to the new Deacon. He'll let me take up my craft again, if I pay enough wax to St Cuthbert's altar.'

'Won't you try to be a merchant again?'

Master Reid shook his head vigorously. 'I'll stick to the trade I ken. I can sell most of the flour that's lying underneath the bed, and live off that. Then I'll lie quiet till the Castle's taken. It'll all come right in the end.'

'And you'll marry Elspeth,' thought David, and clenched his fists in his lap. Master Reid put a hand on his shoulder and said, 'You needna go till you're ready, Davy. I'd be glad to have you stay a wee while.'

David hunched his shoulders. What was the point of staying? Best to say a quick good-bye to Elspeth, and Father Anthony, and Henry Reid, and buy a horse to take him to Leith. He had nothing to hope for from the new Archbishop. His family would want him back in Bordeaux, and the sooner he began his new studies the better. His heart sank as he thought about Elspeth.

'I'll stay, thank you,' he said. 'But only for a few days.'

At the end of a week he was still there. Every day he went with Master Reid to eat his dinner at Widow Brown's, and after the first week she stopped asking him if he had yet managed to find a good horse.

She had become once more the plump, white-coifed woman that David had first met. She treated Elspeth well, but she was mistress in her own kitchen and left them in no doubt as to who had cooked the steaming stews and fish-pies she set before them.

'Would you believe it, Davy,' said Master Reid, as they left the widow's house one afternoon, 'she takes a wee bit meat that wouldna cover a groat, and she can turn it into a feast fit for Linlithgow Palace. It'll be a lucky man that gets to be her next husband.'

David thought he heard a note of regret in Master Reid's voice. He was even more surprised at the brisk way that Madge Brown put her days in the plague-camp behind her. She swept and cleaned her house, and put her linen to air in the spring sunshine; she set Master Reid and David to work and made them tear down the boards nailed across the shutters, and re-plaster her walls that were scorched and grimy from the fires of the city cleansers.

Once she caught David staring at her and read his thoughts too clearly. She smiled in a crooked, ironical way. 'Laddie, do you think we ought to weep for our dead for ever? The world would come to an end yon way.'

After a moment's shocked silence he smiled back at her, and went on daubing white plaster on the wall.

No one except the forty Castilians passed up Castle Wynd, but the rest of the town was still disturbed by brawls between the Castilians and the young craftsmen. Widow Brown never went through the streets herself or sent Elspeth for water until the afternoon, when David or Master Reid could walk beside them.

Once when Elspeth and David were returning from the public well, Elspeth stopped to speak to a blacksmith's wife by the Mercat Cross. 'On your way, David,' she said teasingly, 'it's women's matters we're to talk about.'

David said doubtfully, 'Will you be all right?'

'Of course! I'll cry across the street to you if the Castilians come.'

He walked the few yards to the widow's house and poured the water into the wooden barrels beside the cellar door. As he mounted the forestair he was surprised to hear laughter and giggles coming from the hall. He scraped the door loudly across the threshold, and blinked, trying not to see what he did see: Widow Brown sitting on the carved arm of her late husband's chair, cutting Master Reid's beard.

Neither Master Reid nor the widow showed any confusion, although David flushed with embarrassment.

'You didna ken that Madge was a barber, did you?' chuckled Henry Reid. 'You – och, woman, you nipped my chin!'

David went outside to meet Elspeth. When they entered the beard-cutting was finished. He did not say anything about it to Elspeth.

By the end of May, Master Reid had begun to arrive for his dinner soon after breakfast. In the evenings he sat in front of his own fire uttering loud sighs. David, fiercely whittling a piece of wood with his notched dagger, pretended not to notice, until one night Henry Reid suddenly said, 'What's the date, Davy?'

'The twenty-ninth of May. It's a year today that Norman Leslie killed Archbishop Beaton.'

The thought sobered them both for a moment. Then Master Reid began to sigh again. 'In two days we'll be into June. Davy, I'm sore-hearted. I dinna ken what to do.'

David stood up in his agitation. 'You promised Elspeth! What will she do if you don't marry her?'

'I ken, I ken,' groaned Master Reid. 'I'll not go back on my word. But I must have been doited! And Madge canna understand why I'm so blate to speak my mind. Holy

Mother, I'd pay a double dowry to any well-set-on youngster that would marry Elspeth.'

During the next fortnight Widow Brown began to ask why David and Master Reid looked so long-faced when they came to her table. Was her food no longer to their taste? If they did not like it, she hinted, they could make do for themselves at home.

Master Reid immediately became very gay, but David continued to show a gloomy face, and one day the widow said sharply that she would bear it no longer.

'Take Elspeth for a walk to the sea,' she ordered him. 'It's Sunday, and even if not, I'd rather waste good working-time than have such dreich looks in my house.'

They walked aimlessly down to the harbour and looked at the pile of stones and mouldering reed-thatch where they had once lived. Grass had sprung up between the boulders. Without saying a word they turned their backs on it and walked across the East Bents, between the drying nets.

'Why are you so sad, David?'

He kicked at the tufts of marram grass. 'I think I must go away soon.'

Elspeth slipped her arm into his. 'Before the end of the month?' He knew she was thinking of her marriage. His voice choked in his throat. 'Elspeth –' But what could he say? 'Yes, soon,' he repeated fiercely.

The bell for vespers began to chime from St Nicholas's Hospital. They crossed the Kinness Burn and walked back to the harbour beside the Priory wall. 'Ought I to tell her about the widow?' David asked himself. 'But he's going to marry Elspeth. He said he would. I mustn't tell her.'

At the Sea Port of the Priory, where the mill-stream flowed into the harbour, an elm-tree nodded over the wall.

Its upper branches were full of shrieking, indignant birds; starlings and field-sparrows swooped round the crown of the tree as a small creature wriggled up the trunk.

Elspeth stood on tiptoe. 'Mahound!' she cried. 'Mahound, come down to me, my doo!' The monkey gibbered back at her and swung on to the top of the wall. Elspeth held out her arms. 'Jump, my honey!' she implored. Mahound slithered down the wall and leapt on to her shoulders.

'David, look how thin he is!'

The fine scarlet jacket had gone but there was a tattered leather belt still buckled round his waist. Elspeth buried her face in Mahound's brown fur, while he bounced up and down uttering shrill screams.

'Do you think he escaped when the court left St Andrews, David? He must have lived all winter in the Priory barns. Mahound, my doo, how happy I am!' Elspeth began to cry with joy. 'Wait till I tell Harry Reid. He must let me keep him. Och, he will, won't he, David?'

David took her back to the widow's house. He left Elspeth telling her story to the two adults, and slipped away unnoticed. Feeling bitter and depressed, he walked along the Swallowgate to the empty plague-camp, and round the outer circuit of the town to the Marketgate Port. His walk was almost a run, but he could not shake off his unhappy thoughts.

He found a large crowd in Holy Trinity kirkyard, and more to distract himself than out of curiosity, he joined them. The church doors were open and people were passing in and out.

David edged his way towards the south door. 'What's happening?' he asked a young man in a student's gown.

'Oh, the same as usual. The Castilians have sent their preachers to argue with the University doctors. There's a new one today. He used to be one of the Cardinal's notaries. Fancy a priest speaking against the Kirk! His name is Knox.'

David pushed into the body of the church. The floors and galleries were crowded, and close to the altar rail near the pulpit, David saw a cluster of black University gowns and caps. There was a loud babble of conversation, but the preacher's voice rose above it all.

For a few moments David stood still and listened. The voice came from a swarthy, bearded face. It rose and fell with loud ejaculations, and it spoke of tyranny, and anti-Christ, and the reign of men of blood who had perverted the sacrifice of the mass.

There were angry cries from some of the congregation, but the preacher seemed to enjoy them. He wagged his finger at the University men, while the priests muttered to each other.

'Martin would have liked this,' thought David. He tried to follow the argument: something about the Woman of Babylon and the true Spouse of Christ. His mind refused to take it in. He turned away full of weariness and disgust at what had happened in the past year. He felt a touch on his arm.

'You here, David?' smiled Father Anthony. His face had filled out and he stood upright, like a man in vigorous health.

'He will be burnt,' said David, as they walked out of the church together.

'What, Knox? Oh, no. The roof has begun to fall.'

David thought it was a strange thing to say. 'It means no more to me than it ever did. My mind is full of other things.' He flushed, afraid of sounding arrogant.

'For your sake, I am glad. Your work is in France. When do you leave?'

The question seemed to clear David's mind. He pushed aside the heartache and worry that had sent him walking so furiously round the town. 'Very soon. Next week, on Thursday morning.' He took a deep breath. At last he had made up his mind.

'It's strange how our lives repeat themselves,' said the canon. 'I've the same news for you today as I brought in November. The *Giroflée* is in port.'

He laughed as David took to his heels – along Marketgate, down Foul Waste, and into Northgate. He had just stopped to get his breath by the Fish Cross, before his final spurt down to the harbour, when Elspeth appeared and waved to him.

David stood panting for a moment and then walked towards her. Her eyes were brilliant with excitement. 'David, I went back to Master Reid's house when you left us and there were two strangers waiting for you. I couldna right make out what they said, but I think they've come from the harbour.'

'Who are they?'

'I'm not sure. A man and a woman. The woman said – I think – that her name is Berthe. The man's her husband.'

'Jacques!' yelled David. 'My father's chief warehouseman.'

Why on earth had Jacques come on the *Giroflée*? He was responsible for loading her cargo; he had never sailed with it before. And Berthe – why had she come? He had asked his father to help the Binnies, perhaps to buy them a house in St Andrews. He would not send Jacques and Berthe to see to that. They must have come because – ruthlessly, he told himself not to be a fool.

'Do you know why they're here?'

Elspeth flushed and grew pale again. 'I couldna take

their meaning. The man speaks only French and the woman's not much better. She kept on saying, "If *la grand'mère* permits".' Elspeth stumbled over the French words.

'What else?'

'I think she said something – oh, David, I think she said something about taking me to Bordeaux!' Elspeth hid her face in her hands, and burst into tears and laughter at the same time. 'But there's Harry Reid. What will he do if I dinna marry him?'

David pulled her hands from her face. 'You must have noticed,' he said, in an urgent voice, forgetting that he had prayed before that Elspeth would notice nothing. 'He'll be all right.'

'You mean Harry and Widow Brown?' David nodded.

'Well,' said Elspeth, and they smiled at each other. Then Elspeth cried in sudden panic. 'Maybe I've misheard her, David. Maybe that's not what the Frenchwoman said at all.'

'Let's go and find out.' David took Elspeth by the hand and they ran down the street towards the bakehouse.

A few days later the *Giroflée* was lying outside St Andrews harbour, and the sailors were hauling up the yards. As they shook out the sails, the steeples of the town disappeared behind the canvas. Berthe and Jacques went down to their cabin and David waved his cap for the last time to Master Reid and the widow, who were watching from the quay. He was not sure if they could see him.

'St Leonard's, St Salvator's, Holy Trinity, St Rule's, and the nine pinnacles of the Cathedral,' he murmured. 'We'll go to the other side if you want to see them again.'

Elspeth shook her head as she clutched Mahound,

perched dangerously on the deck-rail. 'I'll not look back till we're past Fife Ness.' She pointed at the headland. 'What a lot of ships! Is that the French king's fleet?'

On the horizon they counted twenty-one war-galleys advancing towards St Andrews Bay. They could see their oars flashing in the sun.

'Yes, it must be.' David turned towards the Castle and saw tiny figures thronging the sea-rampart. The French fleet had been sighted from land as well.

'That's the end of the Castilians,' said Elspeth in a low voice. 'More fighting and men being killed.'

David put his arm around her. 'Don't think about it. It's a new life, Elspeth. I've so many things to tell you about Bordeaux.'

Her face brightened and David wondered once again what he would have done if his father had obeyed his instructions about the Binnies. Jacques had brought him a very angry letter from his father. He winced as he remembered the unkind phrases: 'selfish popinjay'; 'disowning your own cousin'; 'our duty to look after the child ... if the grand-mother will permit'.

No doubt there would be more severe words waiting for him in Bordeaux. It would be difficult to explain why he had changed. But Elspeth was worth it. His arm went round her more tightly.

As they leant against the rail a flat, hard shape pressed against him inside his doublet: Father Anthony's book of medical sketches, his present when they said good-bye. For one moment he thought of another book, lying next to Martin's body, ten feet under the lime-choked soil near the Swilcan Burn. A cold chill went through him; then he thrust the memory away. Not that. Some day there would be better things to remember about Martin, when he could bear to think about him.

'It's a new life,' he repeated to himself firmly. Above their heads the sails began to creak and strain.

'There's a grand breeze,' said Elspeth. 'We're moving. David, how long will it take us to reach Bordeaux?'

ABOUT THE AUTHOR

Iona McGregor's early life was spent in Egypt and India, before her family settled in Perthshire. After the war she lived in England, attending Bristol University and spending most of her holidays with her grandmother in St Andrews while her parents were in Germany with the Control Commission. After taking her degree she worked for several years as a sub-editor on the *Dictionary of the Older Scottish Tongue* at the School of Scottish Studies in Edinburgh. She now teaches classics and lives in Edinburgh; although her home is in the New Town she has a special interest in the Old Town which was the background for her first book. AN EDINBURGH REEL*. Her hobbies include digging (especially Romano-British sites), indoor gardening, and collecting books on Scottish social history. The latter interest is reflected in her first four novels, a linked sequence featuring members of the same family over three centuries of Scottish history. In THE SNAKE AND THE OLIVE*, however, she turned her attention to the island of Cos in ancient Greece, to tell the story of Hippocrates the physician.

HEARD ABOUT THE PUFFIN CLUB

... it's a way of finding out more about Puffin books and authors, of winning prizes (in competitions), sharing jokes, a secret code, and perhaps seeing your name in print! When you join you get a copy of our magazine, *Puffin Post*, sent to you four times a year, a badge and a membership book.

For details of subscription and an application form, send a stamped addressed envelope to:

The Puffin Club Dept A
Penguin Books Limited
Bath Road
Harmondsworth
Middlesex UB7 ODA

and if you live in Australia, please write to:

The Australian Puffin Club
Penguin Books Australia Limited
P.O. Box 257
Ringwood
Victoria 3134